On
EARTH
AS IT IS IN
HEAVEN

ON EARTH AS IT IS IN HEAVEN

HOW THE LORD'S PRAYER TEACHES US TO PRAY MORE EFFECTIVELY

WARREN W. WIERSBE

BakerBooks

a division of Baker Publishing Group
Grand Rapids, Michigan

© 2010 by Warren W. Wiersbe

Published by Baker Books
a division of Baker Publishing Group
P.O. Box 6287, Grand Rapids, MI 49516-6287
www.bakerbooks.com

Printed in the United States of America

Library of Congress Cataloging-in-Publication Data
Wiersbe, Warren W.
     On earth as it is in heaven : how the Lord's prayer teaches us to pray more effectively / Warren W. Wiersbe.
        p.   cm.
     ISBN 978-0-8010-7219-2 (pbk.)
     1. Lord's prayer. 2. Prayer—Christianity. I. Title
BV230.W493 2010
248.3'2—dc22   2009035429

10   11   12   13   14   15   16   7   6   5   4   3   2   1

Dedicated to that faithful remnant of Christian believers
(often unrecognized and underappreciated)
whose prayers glorify God, overcome the enemy,
hasten the spread of the gospel of Jesus Christ,
and build his church around the world.

Thank you!
Don't stop praying!

What would happen to the Church if the Lord's Prayer became a test for membership as thoroughly as the Creeds have been?

P. T. Forsyth
The Soul of Prayer

Contents

Contents

Preface

We should always begin with the basics, the fundamentals.

Writers take the letters of the alphabet, combine them into words and the words into sentences and paragraphs, and produce what we call "literature"—essays, poetry, learned dissertations, news stories, jokes, and advertising.

Painters take dabs of color from their palettes and put them in the right places on their canvases, and we call it "art."

Composers take the notes of the musical scale, arrange them into chords and the chords into melodies, and give us overtures, ballads, hymns, and advertising jingles.

The same principle applies to our praying. Just as a baby cries for his or her parents, the new believer cannot help but cry out, "Abba, Father" (Gal. 4:6). Nevertheless, as babies grow into childhood and beyond, they learn that there's a fascinating yet complicated communications system among humans, and little by little they speak words and build sentences. The same holds true for believers.

If we want to keep maturing in the Christian life, we must be serious about developing our prayer life. To do this, we must know and respond to the basic elements of prayer. Some of these elements are found in the familiar Lord's Prayer recorded in Matthew 6:9–13. My goal in this book is to explain and apply these elements so that you may become excited about praying and mature in your personal prayer ministry.

Martin Luther said that "the ancients ably defined prayer an *Ascensus mentis ad Deum*, a climbing up of the heart unto God."[1] I trust that the Lord will use this book to encourage you to climb higher spiritually and experience a more satisfying and effective prayer life.

"Not to want to pray, then, is the sin behind sin," wrote P. T. Forsyth, "and it ends in not being able to pray."[2]

What a tragic judgment!

Measuring a Miracle

Prayer is a miracle, and the sooner you realize this fact, the sooner prayer ceases to be a dull routine or a religious burden. It becomes an exciting adventure that molds your life and the lives of those for whom you pray. If prayer is a neglected or ignored discipline in your life, then it's time you attempted to measure this miracle and discover what you are missing.

Question: What is God looking for in today's world?
Answer: He is looking for the same things he's been looking for from the beginning of salvation history.

- He is seeking the lost (Luke 19:10)
- He is seeking true worshipers (John 4:23)
- He is seeking spiritual fruit (Luke 13:7; John 15:1–8)
- He is seeking people to stand in the gap (Ezek. 22:30)
- He is seeking intercessors (Isa. 59:16)

Seven hundred years before Jesus was born, Isaiah wrote that the Lord was "astonished that there was no one to intercede." What must God think today when he sees how few people set aside time for intercessory prayer? Or when he listens to a worship service, what does he think when he hears prayers for the offering and the sermon but not for the needs of the church family, the leaders of the nation, or the missionaries the church helps to support? Is God astonished? Are we astonished and convicted because of this neglect of prayer in our homes and churches? After all, the members of the early church "devoted themselves" to prayer (Acts 2:42), and their spiritual leaders focused their ministries on the Word of God and prayer (Acts 6:4). Prayer isn't an option; it's an obligation and an opportunity for us to glorify God's name and receive his blessing. It's also an opportunity to participate in miracles.

A pastor was asked about the prayer ministry in the church he served, and he replied, "We're not into that." His answer was quite different from that of Charles Haddon Spurgeon who, when asked the reason for God's blessing on the Metropolitan Tabernacle ministry, replied, "My people pray for me." Like the apostle Paul, Spurgeon wasn't ashamed to ask people to pray for him. He knew he needed it. We need it too. Prayer isn't a luxury; it's a necessity.

If prayerlessness is one of our sins, this is a good time to confess it. If our church family needs to return to praying, let's ask the Lord what he wants us to do to change things. Are the priorities of our churches and of our individual lives the same as those of our great God? If not, what should we do about it?

David had the right viewpoint when he wrote, "You, God, are my God, earnestly I seek you; I thirst for you, my whole being longs for you, in a dry and parched land where there is no water" (Ps. 63:1).

In our individual lives and in our congregations, we need to recover not only the basics in the practice of prayer but also a deeper understanding of the greatness of prayer. Prayer is a miracle, and it's difficult to measure a miracle; but that shouldn't keep us from personally experiencing the miracle of answered prayer.

That people like us on earth can speak to the Lord in heaven is remarkable; that the Lord pays attention to what we say *and acts on our behalf* is also remarkable. What an astounding thing that Almighty God works on our behalf. The Father hears us and knows our needs even before we ask (Matt. 6:8). The Son intercedes for us and knows exactly how we feel in every situation (Rom. 8:34; Heb. 4:14–16). The Holy Spirit intercedes for us and directs our requests according to the will of God (Rom. 8:26–27). When we pray, we become part of God's miracle work on earth because he is a great God! The bigger prayer is in our lives, the smaller our burdens and battles will appear and the greater our blessings will become.

Not only does prayer connect us with a great God, but the very privilege of prayer is ours at a great price. Jesus Christ had to suffer and die on the cross to make it possible for us to approach the throne of grace to worship and to pray (Heb. 10:19–25). When he finished his redemptive work on earth, Jesus arose from the dead, ascended to the Father in heaven, and began his work of intercession on our behalf. To neglect prayer is to cheapen everything Jesus accomplished for us at Calvary and is doing for us now in glory.

Prayer is a great experience because it is backed up by great promises that never fail. Ever since people began to "call on the name of the LORD" (Gen. 4:26), believers have been claiming God's great promises. "The LORD is near to all who call on him, to all who call on him in truth" (Ps. 145:18). We may pray in solitude, but we are never alone because Jesus is with us. "Let us then approach God's throne of grace with confidence, so that we may receive mercy and find grace to help us in our time of need" (Heb. 4:16). "If any of you lacks wisdom, you should ask God, who gives generously to all without finding fault, and it will be given to you" (James 1:5). That promise helped me during my years of university and seminary studies, and I still claim it as I study God's Word today.

The most important "great thing" about prayer is that, when God answers, it brings great glory to his name. Jesus told his disciples, "And I will do whatever you ask in my name, so that the Father may be glorified in the Son" (John 14:13). No Christian believer can take credit for the miracle of answered prayer, whether that answer is the healing of the sick, the providing of employment, the conversion of the lost, or the solving of a difficult problem. "We do not know what to do," King Jehoshaphat prayed, "but our eyes are on you" (2 Chron. 20:12; see also Heb. 12:2).

God answers prayer, not just to meet the needs of his burdened children but to bring glory to his name through the answers. That's one reason why God permits difficulties in our lives, so that his ministry to us will reveal his power and glory to those who are watching. Do we pray only to have our needs met and our wants supplied as soon as possible, or do we pray because we want to see Jesus glorified on earth? Are we willing to suffer or even to fail if this will honor the Lord in a greater way?

> This is the confidence we have in approaching God: that if we ask anything according to his will, he hears us.
>
> 1 John 5:14

Because they don't realize how awesome prayer is, many individual believers and even entire congregations neglect prayer, some to the point of ignoring it completely. (As the pastor mentioned above said, "We're not into that.") Over a century ago, near the close of his ministry, the noted Scottish preacher Alexander Whyte (1837–1921) preached a series of twenty-six messages on prayer to his people at Free St. George's in Edinburgh, Scotland. He concluded the first sermon with these words:

This, then, is the very topmost glory, and the very supremest praise of God—the men, from among men, that He takes, and makes them Kings and Priests unto God. Let all such men magnify their office; and let them think and speak and sing magnificently of their God![3]

Near the close of the fourth message he said:

Prayer, my brethren, is princely work—prayer, that is, like Jacob's prayer at the Jabbock. Prayer, at its best, is the noblest, the sublimest, the most magnificent, and stupendous act that any creature of God can perform on earth or in heaven.[4]

Read that quotation again and ponder it. Then read about Jacob's experience at Jabbock recorded in Genesis 32. Do we really see prayer as a royal privilege and a princely ministry, as well as a wrestling with God (see Col. 4:12–13), or is prayer only a dull routine for us? Can we learn to pray so that our praying is noble, sublime, magnificent, and stupendous? Of course, Alexander Whyte wasn't referring to the words we speak, because the power of our prayers isn't measured by our vocabulary. If our praying calls attention to itself or our abilities instead of glorifying God, something is radically wrong. Charles Spurgeon told of a ministerial student in his Pastor's College who began his prayer, "O Thou that art encinctured with an auriferous zodiac."[5] The young man got everybody's attention except God's.

To be gripped by the miraculous magnificence of prayer means to be humbled and broken, deeply grateful for the privilege of access into the presence of the Almighty. It means following the example of the publican and crying out for help, not bragging about our achievements as the Pharisee did (Luke 18:9–14). It means depending wholly on the grace of God and not being ashamed to admit it.

The prayer pattern that Jesus gave his disciples, what we call the Lord's Prayer, is the model for us to follow.[6] Jesus

15

said, "This, then, is how you should pray" (Matt. 6:9). That sounds like a commandment, doesn't it?

After a morning worship service where I had been the guest preacher, I asked one of the elders, "Do you ever include the Lord's Prayer in your congregational worship?"

"No, we don't," he replied.

When I asked him why, he said, "When you recite the same words week after week, they can become stale and meaningless." Then I reminded him that we had sung one of the "praise choruses" eight times during the service, but apparently his statement didn't apply to music.

Most congregations have probably never heard of *The Teaching of the Twelve Apostles*, also known as the *Didache* ("The Teaching"), perhaps the oldest non-canonical Christian book we have. The *Didache* makes it clear that the early church always used the Lord's Prayer in its public worship services and did not permit unbelievers to join in the praying. The *Didache* also exhorts all believers to pray the Lord's Prayer three times a day. Of course, the writer assumed that the words would come from the worshipers' hearts and not just from their memories.

The more familiar version of the Lord's Prayer is recorded in Matthew 6:9–13.

> Our Father in heaven, hallowed be your name, your kingdom come, your will be done, on earth as it is in heaven. Give us today our daily bread. And forgive us our debts, as we also have forgiven our debtors. And lead us not into temptation, but deliver us from the evil one.

This prayer is at the heart of the Sermon on the Mount and is preceded by two warnings from our Savior: don't use your prayers to show off how religious you are (6:5–6), and don't just "babble" a lot of meaningless words (6:7–8). Get to the point! It's the strength of our faith and not the length of our prayers that pleases him. Yes, some long prayers are recorded in the Bible (see 2 Chronicles 6, Ezra 9, Nehemiah 9, and Daniel 9), but there are many more short prayers that God heard and answered (e.g., "Lord, save me!" [Matt. 14:30]).

The Lord's Prayer contains six requests, and we will study them in this book. Since the days of the church fathers, it's been pointed out that the first three requests in this prayer focus on matters that especially concern God—the glory of his name, the coming of his kingdom, and the accomplishing of his will—while the last three requests deal with the needs of the one who is praying—the necessities of life, personal forgiveness of sin, and victory over trial and temptation.[7] The prayer asks the Father to forgive the sins of the past, to provide what we need for the present day (both physical and spiritual), and to guide us in the future as we anticipate the coming of Christ's kingdom. Just about every prayer burden we might have, either for ourselves or for others, can fit into each of these six requests.

We must examine our own praying in light of the characteristics of the Lord's Prayer. To begin with, the plural pronouns in the prayer (*our, we,* and *us*) indicate that *the Lord's Prayer is a family prayer.* We may pray in solitude, but we never really pray alone, for as the people of God we belong to each other and we affect each other. It isn't wrong to pray about personal needs. The Scriptures record many personal prayers where *I, my,* and *me* predominate, including David's psalms and the prayers of Jesus and Paul. The plural pronouns in the Lord's Prayer remind us that we belong to a great family of faith and *we must never ask anything for ourselves that would adversely affect our Christian brothers and sisters in the church at large.* I will say more about this in coming pages.

17

The Lord's Prayer was given to *those who have been born into God's family through faith in Jesus Christ.* I'm not suggesting that God never responds mercifully to the cries of those outside his family, because his common grace extends to all creation and all humanity (Matt. 5:43–45; Rom. 2:4). Jesus originally preached the Sermon on the Mount as an ordination sermon for his disciples, but a great crowd of outsiders was also present (Matt. 5:1–2; see Luke 11:1–4).

The Lord's Prayer is not only a family prayer, it's a *balanced* prayer. In it you find requests that relate to the past ("forgive us our debts"), the present ("Give us today our daily bread"), and the future ("your kingdom come"). Some requests relate to the program of God and others to the needs of God's people. Too often our prayers are focused primarily on what we need rather than on what God wants to give or do.

This prayer is simple and to the point, and there is no needless repetition, the very practice Jesus warned about in Matthew 6:7–8. Jesus rebuked the teachers of the law who "for a show [made] lengthy prayers" (Mark 12:40). I recall preaching at a church in Northern Ireland where an elder stood and prayed at great length. As he journeyed through Scripture, I was worried that my passport might run out before he ended. In one of his public meetings evangelist D. L. Moody asked a man to pray, and the man prayed for so long that Moody interrupted him and said to the crowd, "As our brother finishes his prayer, let's sing a hymn." That helped to save the meeting and perhaps even some lost souls.

Finally, the Lord's Prayer is part of what we call the Sermon on the Mount, which means that *effective prayer is linked to a dedicated and obedient life.* In this sermon Jesus emphasizes true godliness as opposed to the artificial piety of the religious leaders of that day. "For I tell you that unless your righteousness surpasses that of the Pharisees and the teachers of the law, you will certainly not enter the kingdom of heaven" (Matt. 5:20). The emphasis is on building godly character (Matt. 5:1–16) and maintaining an obedient heart (5:21–48), not on impressing the spectators.

In the Jewish tabernacle, and then in the temple, there stood before the veil an altar that was only three feet high and eighteen inches square, completely covered with gold. It was the altar of incense on which a very special mixture of spices was burned by a priest each morning and each evening (Exod. 30:1–10, 34–38). The ascending smoke of the fragrant incense typified the prayers of the priests and people as they ascended to the Lord at the beginning and ending of each day (Ps. 141:2). Zechariah the priest was performing this ritual when the angel appeared to him and told him he would have a son (Luke 1:5–25).

The golden altar was the smallest piece of holy furniture in the sanctuary, *and yet it helped to make possible the nation's communion with the Lord.* Without the privilege of praying to God, the people of Israel would have been unable to tell him their needs and burdens and ask for his help. Prayer was the key that opened and closed each day, a good example for us to follow.

Like that golden altar, the Lord's Prayer isn't long and imposing, but it is very precious. You can pray this prayer reverently in a minute or less; but like the incense altar, this prayer isn't measured by its extent but by its content and intent. It's doubtful that Jesus gave us this prayer simply to recite, but rather to be used as a model or pattern, a "divine agenda," to guide us in our own praying so we don't ramble, waste words, and miss the requests that are really important.

"We do not know what we ought to pray for," Paul confesses in Romans 8:26, but then he encourages us to trust the Holy Spirit to guide us. I have learned that the Spirit can use the pattern of the Lord's Prayer to remind me of what I should bring to the throne of grace. As we meditate on this prayer, we will discover how it relates to the personal needs all believers have as we live and serve in this "present evil age" (Gal. 1:4), where God's name is not being revered but blasphemed. While he reigns in heaven, he isn't always allowed to rule on earth, and his will is ignored. God's rich provisions for human life are wasted and destroyed, and there are millions of hungry people looking for bread. We all sin and need forgiveness, and we are prone to listen to the tempter, rebel, and go astray.

In short, all of us as God's children need to allow the Holy Spirit to use this prayer in our lives so that we might please the Father, become more like the Son, and be used of the Holy Spirit to make a difference in this world.

While reading a devotional book prepared especially for ministers, I was introduced to Martin Luther's barber, Peter Beskendorf. Peter asked Luther for some practical guidance for private prayer, and Luther wrote for him (and us) "A Simple Way to Pray." He began with the Lord's Prayer and briefly explained how each petition may be expanded effectively into personal prayer. "For to this day," wrote Luther, "I drink of the Lord's Prayer like a child; drink and eat like an old man; I can never get enough of it. To me it is the best of all prayers."[8]

Of course, his words are meaningless to people who don't pray at all, except in emergencies or when conscripted to pray at a public meeting. Luther's love for the Lord's Prayer is equally a mystery to people who pray routinely or carelessly, just to "finish their daily devotions." But Luther's words thrill the hearts of Christian believers who dwell "in the shelter of the Most High" (Ps. 91:1) and know what it means to "draw near to God with a sincere heart in full assurance of faith" (Heb. 10:22).

To maturing children of God, prayer is a moment-by-moment adventure into the will of God, the character of God, and the blessing of God. Christians who pray are always learning more about the Lord and themselves. Their Christian walk is a constant fellowship in the things of the Spirit. No matter what the circumstances, they speak to the Lord from their hearts and he speaks to them from his Word. Praying means participating in God's miraculous work in this world and letting him receive all the glory. Prayer is the most important thing in their life.

One day when we are in glory, we will see how the Lord used the church's prayers to accomplish his will on earth. Meanwhile, even though we can't measure the miracle of prayer, we can still experience it; so let's begin.

Relationship I

"*Our* Father *in heaven*"

On April 26, 1862, author and editor Thomas Wentworth Higginson of Worcester, Massachusetts, received a letter from an aspiring young poet named Emily Dickinson, who lived in Amherst. Referring to her parents and siblings, she wrote, "They are religious, except me, and address an eclipse, every morning, whom they call their Father."

During an eclipse, the light is temporarily obscured, which suggests that Emily wasn't really sure about God. But "God is light; in him there is no darkness at all" (1 John 1:5). He is "the Father of the heavenly lights, who does not change like shifting shadows" (James 1:17).

After teaching a Bible class of college and university students, I was approached by a young man who said, "You claim that God is a father, right?" I replied, "Yes, that's what the Bible teaches." He gave me an angry look and said, "If God is like *my* father, I'm not interested." Before I could respond, he turned and walked defiantly out of the room.

The Lord's Prayer begins with *relationships*—our relationship to God ("Our *Father*") and our relationship to God's people ("*Our* Father"), the latter of which we'll take up in the next chapter. Of course, God is spirit and therefore has no body (John 4:24), which means that the title *Father* has nothing to do with gender. We must not refer to God as *it* because God is a person. Using the known to explain the unknown, the Holy Spirit chose *Father* and *Son* when referring to the first two persons in the Godhead (Matt. 28:19; Luke 4:18; see also Isa. 61:1–2).

✠✠✠✠✠

The principal name of God in the Old Testament is LORD, translated in some versions as "Jehovah" or "Yahweh." God's relationship to Israel is occasionally compared to that of a father who loves and cares for his family. He called Israel his "firstborn son" (Exod. 4:22) and "the children of the LORD" (Deut. 14:1; see Isa. 1:2; Jer. 31:9). He compared Israel's exodus from Egypt and their wilderness journey to a child being picked up and carried by his father (Deut. 1:31; Jer. 31:32; Hos. 11:1). "Is he not your Father, your Creator, who made you and formed you?" asked Moses (Deut. 32:6; see also Isa. 63:16; 64:8; Mal. 2:10).

Psalms 78, 89, 106, and 136 record some of the works of the Lord that he performed for his people Israel, and he treated them as a father does his children. Not only did he protect them and provide for them in Egypt and in the wilderness, but he disciplined them so they might learn to obey, and he brought them into the Promised Land and helped them defeat their enemies. He gave them men and women to lead them, and he enabled the people to build cities and to develop the land. Did they deserve these blessings? No more than we deserve the blessings we have in Jesus Christ (Eph. 1:1–14). The heavenly Father loves his children and cares for them.

Most Israelites, however, probably didn't think of Jehovah as a father. Israel's solemn experience at Sinai (where even Moses was frightened; see Heb. 12:21), and God's disciplining of the nation during their wilderness journey, reminded the people that their God didn't tolerate unbelief and disobedience. "God disciplines us for our good, that we may share in his holiness" (Heb. 12:10). He is a Father who is determined that his children will obey him and grow in godly character.

According to the book of Judges, the nation's repeated apostasy got them into trouble, and God allowed the godless Gentile armies to ravage the land and enslave the people. The Lord finally had to send the Assyrians to destroy the northern kingdom of Israel. Then he sent the Babylonians to carry off the people of the southern kingdom of Judah to Babylon, where they were exiled for seventy years. Why? Because "the LORD disciplines those he loves, as a father the son he delights in" (Prov. 3:12). "If I am a father, where is the honor due me?" God asked his people in Malachi 1:6, and he asks that same question of his church today.

During the old covenant period there were certainly individual believers who joyfully recognized the fatherhood of God, accepted his love, and expressed their love to him. "A father to the fatherless" is what David called him (Ps. 68:5). "As a father has compassion on his children, so the LORD has compassion on those who fear him" (Ps. 103:13). We can't read 2 Samuel 7—especially verse 14—without feeling the powerful father/son relationship between David and his God. While Jeremiah's major metaphor is that of a patient and forgiving husband, he also mentions the fatherhood of Jehovah (Jer. 3:4, 19; 31:9).

In Psalm 115, the writer ridicules the Gentiles for their dead idols and rejoices that he knows the true and living God. The psalmist is so overwhelmed at this truth that he writes, "Not to us, LORD, not to us but to your name be the glory, because of your love and faithfulness" (v. 1). A lifeless idol has no glory, but our Father in heaven is "the glorious Father" (Eph. 1:17).

We who have the written Word should know something about this glorious Father. In the Gospels, Jesus Christ gives us a wonderful revelation of God as our Father, a God who is personal and loving. However, like the apostles, we don't always get the message. Philip said, "Lord, show us the Father and that will be enough for us." Our Lord's reply was, "Don't you know me, Philip, even after I have been among you such a long time? Anyone who has seen me has seen the Father" (John 14:8–9). "If you knew me, you would know my Father also" (John 8:19). Nobody else could honestly make that statement.

At the baptism of Jesus, the Father declared from heaven, "This is my Son, whom I love; with him I am well pleased" (Matt. 3:17). "No one has ever seen God, but the one and only Son, who is himself God and is in closest relationship with the Father, has made him known" (John 1:18). It was the Father who assigned the works that Jesus did (John 5:36) and who gave the words that Jesus spoke (John 14:8; 17:10). Jesus was able to say, "I always do what pleases him" (John 8:29).

Jesus said to the Father, "I have manifested Your name to the men whom You gave me out of the world" (John 17:6 NASB, and see v. 26). Because of the seven "I am" statements of Jesus in John's Gospel, some Bible students believe that the "name" Jesus was referring to is I AM (Exod. 3:13–14), but it's more likely that "name" refers to God's character. Jesus is saying to us, "In my life and ministry, I have revealed the Father to you." As we read the four Gospels and look at Jesus, we get better acquainted with the Father and the Son.

Look at Jesus welcoming the children and you see God with a child in his arms. See Jesus at the tomb of his beloved friend Lazarus and you see God with tears running down his face. Watch Jesus cleanse the temple and you behold God with a whip in his hand. Behold Jesus in the upper room, washing his disciples' feet, and you see God humbling himself as the servant of undeserving sinners. You see God with a towel in his hands.

The Son came to glorify the Father (John 13:31–32), and the Spirit came to glorify the Son through his people (John

16:14). When Jesus prayed that the Father would glorify him, he was referring to his resurrection and ascension after he had finished his redemptive work on the cross (John 12:20–29; 17:1). We glorify our Father in heaven by being what Jesus told us to be: salt in a decaying world and light in a dark world (Matt. 5:13–16).

No one must be permitted to take the place of the heavenly Father. "And do not call anyone on earth 'father,' " Jesus instructed his disciples, "for you have one Father, and he is in heaven" (Matt. 23:9). Of course, Jesus wasn't referring to their biological fathers, for it's proper for children to address their parents respectfully as *father* and *mother*, or some version of those titles (mama, papa, daddy, etc.). Some children go through a phase when they think it's smart to address their parents by their first names, a practice that I think is reprehensible and inexcusable.

The point Jesus emphasizes is that the Father in heaven is our sole Master and must not be replaced by the most beloved person on earth. When you read Matthew 23:1–12, you hear Jesus rebuking the Jewish religious leaders who loved to be exalted by the people and called *rabbi* ("my great one"), *father*, or *master*. The apostle Paul called himself *father* when he wrote to the believers in Corinth (1 Cor. 4:15), because he was the human instrument God used to bring them into God's family; *but neither Paul nor any other apostle asked any of the believers to refer to them as* father.

God has placed teachers and spiritual leaders in the churches as the servants of the heavenly Father and his people, and they must not usurp God's authority by controlling the lives of other believers (John 13:12–17; 1 Peter 5:1–7; 3 John 9–11). God's leaders must be servants but not celebrities, directors but not dictators. They must never accept the honor that belongs to God alone. Unfortunately, some of God's people are so immature that they must have "babysitters" or "custodians" to tell them what to do (Gal. 3:23–4:7). They would rather remain "babes" than feed on the Word and exercise themselves in godliness so they might mature and serve others. They forget that Jesus commanded, "Be perfect [mature, complete], therefore, as your heavenly Father is perfect" (Matt. 5:45). We must not allow ourselves to become enslaved to other believers, no matter how exemplary they may be (2 Cor. 11:20). The Father wants us to become mature believers who obey his will and glorify his name.

In the Sermon on the Mount, Jesus mentions the Father seventeen times, and ten of those references include the modifier *heaven* or *heavenly*. When Jesus says "your Father in heaven" or "your heavenly Father," he is emphasizing the high privilege as well as the great responsibility we have as the children of God. Just as our children and grandchildren can bring praise or shame to the family name, so God's children can glorify the Father (Matt. 5:16) or dishonor him and his family. According to Matthew 6, the Father sees all that is happening (vv. 1–4), hears all that is said (vv. 5–6), knows all that is needed (vv. 7–8), and rewards all of his children who have obeyed him (vv. 1–6).

On the morning of his resurrection, Jesus said to Mary Magdalene, "Go . . . to my brothers and tell them, 'I am ascending to my Father and your Father, to my God and your God'" (John 20:17). He did not say, "I am ascending to *our* Father and to *our* God," for the Son's eternal relationship to the Father is unique. Positionally, each believer is "in Jesus Christ" and therefore as near to the Father as Jesus is; but Jesus is still the eternal Son of God, and his oneness with the Father cannot be duplicated in others (see Matt. 11:25–27). We must accept our glorious position in Christ with great gratitude and humility.

Although Israel received many spiritual gifts from God, the blessings he promised Israel were primarily material—a fruitful land, dependable rainfall, health, productive flocks and herds, protection from their enemies, and so forth. The church, on the other hand, has been given no guarantee of material wealth but has been given "every spiritual blessing in Christ" (Eph. 1:3). Israel is identified with the earth, but the church is identified with heaven.

Our Father is in heaven, and therefore our eternal home is in heaven (John 14:1–6). We are pilgrims and strangers on earth because we are citizens of heaven where our Savior is enthroned, and one day he will come to take us home (Phil. 3:20–21). As citizens, our names are permanently written down in heaven because heaven is where we belong (Luke 10:20).

"Since, then, you have been raised with Christ, set your hearts on things above, where Christ is seated at the right hand of God. Set your minds on things above, not on earthly things" (Col. 3:1–2). How can we sincerely pray "Our Father in heaven" if our affection and attention are not focused on heaven? This does not mean we're "so heavenly minded that we're no earthly good"—a phrase D. L. Moody used—but that everything we do on earth is motivated by heaven and the promised return of our Savior. The people of this world look at heaven from earth's point of view, but God's people look at this world from heaven's point of view. This is the way Abraham and Moses lived (Heb. 11:8–16, 24–28), and God blessed them because their attention was heavenward.

What does it mean to walk by faith? It means to obey God's Word in spite of the feelings within us, the circumstances around us, and the consequences before us. The people of Israel saw the Red Sea before them and the Egyptian army behind them, but Moses looked by faith to the Lord above them, and he led the nation safely out of Egypt.

🌷🌷🌷🌷🌷

The phrase "our Father" speaks of God's nearness to us, while the phrase "in heaven" speaks of his distance and difference from us, and both truths are important in the Christian life and must be kept in balance. The technical terms are the *immanence* of God (he is near us) and the *transcendence* of God (he is beyond us). Theologian Millard J. Erickson writes, "The question of whereness does not apply to God. He is not a physical being; hence he does not have spatial dimensions of location and extension."[9] Transcendence means that God is uniquely and wholly "other" than everything else, far above his creation in his being and in his activity. Immanence means that he has chosen to be near to those who trust him and seek to do his will, and he works in and through them.

When King Solomon dedicated the temple in Jerusalem, he prayed, "But will God really dwell on earth? The heavens, even the highest heaven, cannot contain you. How much less this temple I have built!" (1 Kings 8:27). David wrote, "The LORD has established his throne in heaven, and his kingdom rules over all" (Ps. 103:19). "Who is like the LORD our God, the One who sits enthroned on high?" (Ps. 113:5). Moses admonished the Jewish people to fear God and obey him, and then added a very good reason for doing so: "To the LORD your God belong the heavens, even the highest heavens, the earth and everything in it. Yet the LORD set his affection on your ancestors and loved them, and he chose you, their descendants, above all the nations—as it is today" (Deut. 10:14–15).

The Lord is "high" and yet he "stooped down" to love us and choose a people to be his very own. He is transcendent and yet he is also immanent. What a glorious God he is! This was the message at the birth of Christ: "Glory to God in the highest heaven [transcendence] and on earth peace to those on whom his favor rests [immanence]" (Luke 2:14). Jesus is called *Immanuel*, which means "God with us" (Isa. 7:14; Matt. 1:23). Our Lord emphasized this balance when he gave the Great Commission to his disciples: "All authority in heaven and on earth has been given to me. . . . And surely I am with you always, to the very end of the age" (Matt. 28:18, 20). We can enter each day with the assurance that the Lord is on his throne *above us*, providentially guiding us and our circumstances, and that he is also *with us*, giving us the grace we need for each task and challenge.

I might add that congregational worship should keep transcendence and immanence in balance. Biblical worship should begin with transcendence, affirming that the Lord is above us and is in control. Then we should move to immanence, thanking the Lord that he is with us as we leave his sanctuary. The current "buddy-buddy" approach to the Lord is definitely unbiblical. "Abba, Father" is fine for personal devotions but not always for corporate worship. We must first see the Lord "seated on a throne, high and exalted" so that we may truly say, "Woe is me" and "Here am I. Send me!" (Isa. 6:1–8). The prophet Isaiah describes this balance beautifully (57:15):

> For this is what the high and exalted One says—he who lives forever, whose name is holy: "I live in a high and holy place, but also with those who are contrite and lowly in spirit, to revive the spirit of the lowly and to revive the heart of the contrite."

If we enter into his presence with a proud spirit of self-confidence, we will miss the blessing; but if we are bowed and broken before him, he will cleanse us, speak to us, and give us the grace we need to accomplish what he wants us to do. His transcendence and his immanence minister together.

It's unfortunate that most people, including Christian people, rarely talk about heaven until a friend or family member is critically injured or gets sick and dies. We have to experience the worst before we feel free to talk about the best, and that isn't right. I've often reminded people that heaven is not only a *destination*, it's a *motivation*. When you and I are truly motivated by the promise of eternity with God in heaven, it makes a difference in our lives.

The Sermon on the Mount has much to say about heaven. The first blessing Jesus offers us is citizenship in the kingdom of heaven: "Blessed are the poor in spirit, for theirs is the kingdom of heaven" (Matt. 5:3). Our obedience and service on earth glorify the Father in heaven and point others to him (Matt. 5:16). Heaven is "God's throne" (Matt. 5:34) and he gives the orders. "Our God is in heaven; he does whatever pleases him" (Ps. 115:3). The loving way we treat those who oppose and hate us is evidence that we are "children of [our] Father in heaven" (Matt. 5:11–12, 43–45). We may be abused and robbed on earth, but there are rewards in heaven awaiting the faithful (Matt. 6:1). If we have the right values and are generous, we store up "treasures in heaven" (Matt. 6:19–24) that can never be taken from us.

⚜⚜⚜⚜

The fatherhood of God is the basis for the requests in the Lord's Prayer, as it is in every prayer that is truly biblical.

Because God is our Father, we want to glorify him, so we pray, "Hallowed be your name." Every child should want to live to honor the family name.

Birth into the family of God has given us citizenship in the kingdom of God, but the fullness of that kingdom will not be experienced until Jesus returns. "The kingdom of the world has become the kingdom of our Lord and of his Messiah, and he will reign for ever and ever" (Rev. 11:15; see 19:11–21). We pray, "Your kingdom come."

Meanwhile, as we wait for his return, we want to know the Father's will and assist him in accomplishing it on this earth. We are "God's co-workers" (2 Cor. 6:1), partners in doing God's work and accomplishing God's will. As we do his will, he provides for us out of his wealth and we receive our "daily bread."[10] But we also labor with other believers and our fellowship with them is important, so we ask God (and others) to forgive us when we sin and to help us avoid the temptations of the enemy.

It all adds up to this: one of the most important elements of effective praying is a deepening relationship with the Father. This means worshiping the Father, knowing him better through his Word, fellowshiping with him, obeying his will, and seeking to please him.

After all, one day we want to hear him say, "You are my child, whom I love; with you I am well pleased" (see Luke 3:22).

Praise, My Soul, the King of Heaven

Praise, my soul, the King of heaven,
To His feet thy tribute bring;
Ransomed, healed, restored, forgiven,
Evermore His praises sing.
   Alleluia! Alleluia! Praise the everlasting King!

Praise Him for His grace and favor
To our fathers in distress;
Praise Him, just the same as ever,
Slow to chide and swift to bless.
   Alleluia! Alleluia! Glorious is His faithfulness.

Fatherlike, He tends and spares us;
Well our feeble frame He knows;
In His hands He gently bears us,
Rescues us from all our foes.
   Alleluia! Alleluia! Widely yet His mercy flows.

Angels in the height, adore Him;
You behold Him face to face;
Saints triumphant, bow before Him,
Gathered in from every race.
   Alleluia! Alleluia! Praise with us the God of grace!

Henry Francis Lyte

Relationship II

"Our *Father in heaven*"

President Herbert Hoover liked to use the phrase "rugged individualism" to describe the resolute character that helped to build the United States. His successor in office, Franklin Delano Roosevelt, modified the concept when he said, "I believe in individualism . . . up to the point where the individual starts to operate at the expense of society." It's a small step from individualism to selfishness; and when too many people decide to live as they please, the results are likely to be confusion, fragmentation, and possible destruction. We need each other, especially when it comes to the life of prayer.

Each of us is a unique individual, and our individuality is important and valuable because God gave it to us. We must identify it, give thanks for it, and put it to work for the good of others and the glory of God. All of us are made from the dust, but we were cast in different molds. We are the same and yet we are different. It's our individuality that enables each of us to make a special contribution to society, but we must never confuse *individuality* with *individualism*, rugged or otherwise. "True solitude is the home of the person," wrote Thomas Merton, "false solitude the refuge of the individualist."[11]

American naturalist and writer Henry David Thoreau claimed that he "marched to a different drummer." But during the two years, two months, and two days he lived at Walden Pond, he never got very far away from his family home in Concord, Massachusetts. He was a temporary recluse, not a lifelong hermit. Furthermore, Thoreau was able to live at Walden Pond because of his friend Ralph Waldo Emerson. Emerson gave him permission to cut down the trees and build the cabin on his property, and he even loaned Thoreau an axe. "It is difficult to begin without borrowing," Thoreau wrote in *Walden*, and then he boasted that he had returned the axe to Emerson sharper than when he received it.

Thoreau determined to have margins in his life, and it was a wise decision. We all need margins; otherwise, even the people we love may rob us of the room we need for thinking, praying, and growing. But solitude is only one side of the coin. We also need connections, relationships with people who can challenge us, teach us, and encourage us, even if occasionally they irritate us. We have no right to "do our own thing" at the expense of society. This is especially true for those of us who are followers of Jesus Christ. We may not find it difficult to get along with ourselves when we're alone, but how well do we get along with others?

> To live above with saints we love,
> Will certainly be glory.
> To live below with saints we know—
> Well, that's another story.

I learned that bit of doggerel while in seminary, and more than sixty years of Christian life and ministry have convinced me that it's true, especially when we pray. However, we can learn to love the saints below if we will pray for them when we approach the divine throne of grace in heaven.

It's one thing to say that God is *a* Father and quite something else to say that God is *our* Father. The possessive pronoun *our* is clearly plural, so to whom does it refer? The Lord's Prayer is used so widely by people of different beliefs that you might think Jesus gave this prayer to everybody in the world, but he didn't.

Some Bible students believe that the Lord's Prayer is for everybody because God is the "Father" of all human beings. They quote Malachi 2:10 to prove their point: "Do we not all have one Father? Did not one God create us?" But they need to finish the quotation and discover that the verse refers, not to everybody everywhere, but specifically to the nation of Israel: "Why do we profane the covenant of our ancestors by being unfaithful to one another?" As far as I know, the nation of Israel and the church of Jesus Christ are the only people in this world with whom God has made covenants.

However, since God did create the first man and woman, there is a sense in which every human being can claim God as Father not by *salvation* but by *creation*. Moses called him "God of every human spirit" (Num. 16:22; 27:15–17), and Hebrews 12:9 calls him "the Father of spirits." Paul took this approach in his famous address to the Greek philosophers in Athens (Acts 17:22–31), affirming that nobody should *make* gods because the one true God has made all of us. As far as our humanity is concerned, we are "God's offspring" (v. 29). God is the Father of humankind because he is the Creator of humankind.

But being born into the *human* family doesn't automatically make us members of *God's* family, nor does it give us the privilege of prayer. It's by being born again through faith in Jesus Christ the Savior that we become children of God. "For you have been born again, not of perishable seed [human conception] but of imperishable, through the living and enduring word of God" (1 Peter 1:23, and see John 3:1–18).

How do we know we are truly God's children? "The Spirit himself testifies with our spirit that we are God's children" (Rom. 8:16). When we read the Bible, when we share in congregational worship, when we meet another believer, when we do a good deed in the name of Jesus, the Spirit affirms within us that we belong to the family of God.

If God utterly abandoned any part of his creation, including the human family, the result would be decay and death. Paul told the Greek philosophers that it is God who "gives everyone life and breath and everything else" (Acts 17:25). Like a loving father, God cares for his creation. The sun rises on the evil and the good, and the rain falls on the righteous and the unrighteous (Matt. 5:43–45). The Lord gives us "the ability to produce wealth" (Deut. 8:18) so that we can work and eat and pay our bills.

It's because of God's goodness and grace that we have what we need. "God saw everything that he had made, and it was very good" (Gen. 1:31). In spite of what generations of people have done to pollute and waste God's bounteous gifts to us, we can still survive on Planet Earth. Only in this sense is God the Father of humankind.

⚘⚘⚘⚘⚘

The Lord's Prayer doesn't advocate selfish individualism. It doesn't begin with the words "*My* Father"; it begins with "*Our* Father." Our relationship to the Lord is our most important relationship in life. Because we're in fellowship with the Father, we can enjoy fellowship with his children. "If we say we love God yet hate a brother or sister, we are liars. For if we do not love a fellow believer, whom we have seen, we cannot love God, whom we have not seen" (1 John 4:20).

Certainly it's a high privilege for us to belong to the family of God and know the heavenly Father, the glorified Son, and the indwelling Holy Spirit. But with this privilege comes the unavoidable responsibility of calling other believers our brothers and sisters in Christ. That's why we say *our* and *we* and *us* when we pray the Lord's Prayer. To ignore these plural pronouns is to rob ourselves of blessing and to weaken the church.

If we follow our Lord's directions and go into our room and shut the door to pray, there will probably be fewer distractions (Matt. 6:6); but physical separation must not become spiritual and emotional isolation from other people. Jesus prayed in solitude and so should we (Mark 1:35), but praying in solitude is not the same as praying alone. We can never be alone. Wherever I go, the Lord is with me, and I carry in my mind and heart many people who often find their way into my prayers. For some of them, I give thanks and joyfully pray for them (Phil. 1:1–6); for others, I feel pain and ask God to help them and to give me the opportunity to help them. These needy people may interrupt my prayers and send me on an errand.

Let me explain.

Jesus told about a worshiper who brought a gift to the altar, only to discover that, in his mind and heart, he had brought with him a brother who was holding something against him. The worshiper wasn't alone after all! "Go and be reconciled to that person," counseled Jesus; "then come and offer your gift" (Matt. 5:23–26). Repairing a friendship is, in God's sight, as important as offering a valuable sacrifice.

Paul wrote to the men in every Christian congregation, "Therefore I want the men everywhere to pray, lifting up holy hands without anger or disputing" (1 Tim. 2:8). In my imagination I see a man about to lift his hands in prayer, but in his mind's eye he sees a Christian brother standing next to him, a brother with whom he had disputed in a rude and angry way. So the worshiper puts down his hands, goes and finds his brother, apologizes to him, and invites him to return to the prayer meeting with him. Being able to talk to a brother in love is as important as being able to talk to God.

In 1 Peter, the apostle calls to mind the image of a husband during his morning devotions. As he reads his Bible and meditates, he senses that his wife is there with him, and she is quietly weeping. Then he recalls that he had been unkind and inconsiderate toward her, and he knows he can't pray sincerely until the matter is settled. So he leaves the prayer closet, apologizes to his wife, and kisses her, and together they bow and gratefully talk to God (1 Peter 3:7). It's proper for us to tell God how much we love him, but at times telling others that we love them is equally important.

I recall sitting in my study one morning, trying to prepare a sermon, and the well was dry. The fresh breath of the Spirit wasn't blowing. I put my arms on the desk and my head on my arms and began to pray desperately. As I asked the Lord to remove the obstacles, the face of a brother I had offended immediately came to my mind and interrupted my prayer. I phoned the brother, who lived in another city, and apologized for my sin. We prayed together, and the matter was settled. Turning back to my studies, I felt the wind of the Spirit blowing, and the waters began to flow!

God may have to interrupt our prayers occasionally to teach us the important fact that we never pray alone.

Disconnection is a major problem in today's world. Nation fights against nation, race challenges race, the rich take advantage of the poor, the powerful walk on the weak, and "love your neighbor" is forgotten like an old advertising slogan. But while the enemy is trying to wreck society, Jesus Christ and his faithful church are putting people together. "Whoever is not with me is against me," said Jesus, "and whoever does not gather with me scatters" (Matt. 12:30). God's ultimate goal in history is "to bring unity to all things in heaven and on earth under Christ" (Eph. 1:10), *and he will succeed*. In the Ephesian letter, Paul emphasizes the unity of Christ's church and writes about "the whole building" (2:10), "every family" (3:15), and "the whole body" (4:16). He reminds us that the day will come when Jesus Christ will "fill the whole universe" (4:10). Until that happens, our task is to be "gatherers" who are helping to unite things in every aspect of life.

As a Christian, I'm not a physical unit in a religious organization. I'm a living part of a miraculous spiritual unity in Christ—a member of one body (1 Cor. 12:12–14), a stone in one temple (Eph. 2:19–22; 1 Peter 2:4–7), a branch in one vine (John 15:1–9), to name but a few of the New Testament images of the church. All Christians are different, and yet we are all united in Christ. Regardless of race, color, gender, political or economic status, believers are "all one in Christ Jesus" (Gal. 3:26–29). Unity without diversity is uniformity, and diversity without unity is anarchy; but unity and diversity combined by the Holy Spirit in the church will produce a dynamic life of sacrifice and service that can change the world.

The words "Our Father" remind us not to pray selfishly for anything that would hurt or harm another believer or another church. Here's a scene from the New Testament that illustrates what I mean.

Then the mother of Zebedee's sons came to Jesus with her sons and, kneeling down, asked a favor of him [Jesus]. "What is it you want?" he asked. She said, "Grant that one of these two sons of mine may sit at your right and the other at your left in your kingdom." "You don't know what you are asking," Jesus said to them. "Can you drink the cup I am going to drink?" "We can," they answered. Jesus said to them, "You will indeed drink from my cup, but to sit at my right or left is not for me to grant. These places belong to those for whom they have been prepared by my Father." When the ten heard about this, they were indignant with the two brothers. Jesus called them together and said, "You know that the rulers of the Gentiles lord it over them, and their high officials exercise authority over them. Not so with you. Instead, whoever wants to become great among you must be your servant, and whoever wants to be first must be your slave—just as the Son of Man did not come to be served, but to serve, and to give his life as a ransom for many."

Matthew 20:20–28

We can admire a great deal in this event. A mother wanted the very best for her sons, so she humbled herself before the Lord and asked for a favor. Her prayer was specific as she claimed the kingdom promise Christ had spoken earlier (Matt. 19:28). And what were the results of her prayer? Her request was rejected, her sons were rebuked, and the ten other disciples were resentful. Her prayer didn't glorify Jesus; it grieved him. It didn't bring blessing to the twelve; it divided them and created anger and envy. But one good thing came out of the event: we today can learn from it.

James explains what really happened. "What causes fights and quarrels among you? Don't they come from your desires that battle within you? You desire but do not have, so you kill. You covet but you cannot get what you want, so you quarrel and fight. You do not have because you do not ask God. When you ask, you do not receive, because you ask with wrong motives, that you may spend what you get on your pleasures" (James 4:1–3). This passage describes three "wars" that may be going on in our own lives today. We're at war with others because we're at war with ourselves, and we're at war with ourselves because we're at war with God.

Three moving prayers of confession are in the Old Testament—Ezra 9, Nehemiah 9, and Daniel 9—and in each the pronoun *we* is used frequently. Ezra, Nehemiah, and Daniel weren't personally guilty of the sins confessed in these prayers, but they identified themselves with the people who did commit them. Instead of making excuses or blaming others, they came right to the point and said, "We have sinned!" Sin disconnects us from people, but repentance and confession will restore us. Humble prayers build bridges, but selfish prayers tear them down and build barbed wire fences.

I asked a pastor if he ever included any other church in town in his pulpit prayer each Sunday, and he said, "No." When I asked why, he replied, "Most of our members think our church *is* the only church in town." But he did start to pray systematically for the pastors and ministries of other churches, and I think his successor continues to do so. I'm sure many good things have come out of this practice, because when you start praying sincerely for others, you often end up helping them in some way yourself. "Now to him who is able to do immeasurably more than all we ask or imagine, *according to his power that is at work within us*" (Eph. 3:20, emphasis added). The Lord usually starts to answer prayer by working first in the hearts of those who are praying. Jesus instructed his disciples to ask God to send out laborers, and then he sent them out (Luke 10:1–4).

Scripture is filled with examples that illustrate this truth. Abraham interceded for Lot, who was living in Sodom. When Lot was taken captive, God used Abraham to rescue him (Genesis 18–19). Certainly Moses in Midian was praying for his enslaved relatives and friends in Egypt, and God called him to return to Egypt and set them free. Grieved at the sad plight of the Jews in Jerusalem, Nehemiah wept and prayed for them, and the Lord sent him to rebuild Jerusalem and revitalize its citizens (Nehemiah 1). "Well, the least I can do is pray for you," we hear Christians say, but they are dead wrong. *The most we can do is to pray for others, because that's the first step in our getting involved with them to help meet their needs.*

The phrase "love one another" is found at least a dozen times in the New Testament, and prayer is one way we practice that love. Through prayer I can love people miles away, even people I have never met; and if I'm sincerely loving and praying, I will want to help them when I hear about their needs. This is how God turns burdens into blessings and glorifies himself by answering prayer. Granted, some "prayer letters" may have little to do with prayer, but true servants of God aren't ashamed to unburden their hearts with true intercessors.

Open your concordance to *another* and you will learn that "love one another" is but one of more than thirty "one another" statements found in the New Testament.[12] As we obey them, we are obeying the most important "one another" statement of all—"Love one another" (John 13:34–35; 15:12, 17). Christian love isn't a passing emotion. It's a compelling motivation, energized by the Holy Spirit and nurtured by prayer, the Scriptures, congregational worship, and sacrificial service. Christian love means treating others the way the Father treats us; so when we pray "Our Father," we're including both God and others. That's why I say that our relationship to the Father is the most important connection in life, because it determines every other relationship. And the way we treat others helps to determine our relationship to the Father. In the parable of the prodigal son (Luke 15:11–32), the older brother couldn't get along with his father because he refused to accept and forgive his younger brother. The relationships are reciprocal.

From Cain who murdered his brother Abel (Gen. 4:1–16) to Diotrephes who "loved to be first" in the church (3 John 9–10), the Bible honestly records how people have sinned against each other. Our Lord's disciples lived in the presence of the Son of God, and yet they frequently argued over who among them was the greatest. The Corinthian church had the godly apostle Paul as their founder and first pastor, yet the congregation was divided four ways (1 Cor. 1:10–19). The legalistic Galatian Christians were "biting and devouring each other" and "provoking and envying each other" (Gal. 5:15, 26). After listing some of the physical sufferings he had endured in his ministry, Paul wrote, "Besides everything else, I face daily the pressure of my concern for all the churches" (2 Cor. 11:28). It was easier for him to endure shipwreck than to see the people of God destroy the church of God. Every faithful servant of God knows what Paul means.

Why should it be so difficult for us as God's children to love one another as Jesus commanded us to do? For one thing, each church is a family, and the "spiritual children" are at various stages of growth. As in any family, the older must be patient with the younger and help them in their maturing. My wife and I once visited a home where there were five children, ages two to thirteen, and there was a beautiful harmony in that family. The mother told us their "secret": the children were taught to care for each other just as their parents cared for them. That's what makes church eldership a challenge! All the members of the body "should have equal concern for each other" (1 Cor. 12:25). Peter agrees with Paul: "Each of you should use whatever gift you have received to serve others, as faithful stewards of God's grace in its various forms" (1 Peter 4:10).

But there's another reason we should love one another: each individual believer and church family is under attack by the world, the flesh, and the devil (Eph. 2:1–3; James 4:1–10). Cain killed Abel his brother because Cain "belonged to the evil one" (1 John 3:11–15). The Corinthian saints were feuding because some of them were "spiritual babies" and living for the flesh, while others were arrogantly mixing the wisdom of God with the wisdom of this world (1 Cor. 1:18–30). The world, the flesh, and the devil! Had these believers been walking in the Spirit and not gratifying the appetites of the flesh, they would have loved each other and enjoyed a united church family (Gal. 5:16–26).

It's a privilege to call God *Father* and to use that little word *our* to embrace all of God's children. From wherever we pray, we reach up to the throne of heaven and reach out to believers in "every tribe and language and people and nation" (Rev. 5:9). God in heaven is listening, and God's people everywhere are praying "Our Father"—and that includes you and me!

Blest Be the Tie That Binds

Blest be the tie that binds
Our hearts in Christian love:
The fellowship of kindred minds
Is like to that above.

Before our Father's throne
We pour our ardent prayers;
Our fears, our hopes, our aims are one,
Our comfort and our cares.

We share our mutual woes,
Our mutual burdens bear,
And often for each other flows
The sympathizing tear.

When we asunder part,
It gives us inward pain;
But we shall still be joined in heart,
And hope to meet again.

John Fawcett

Worship

"Hallowed be your name"

At the beginning of the Lord's Prayer, the word *Father* indicates *to whom* we pray, and the word *our* refers to those *with whom* we pray, God's worldwide family of faith. Now we must examine our motives and ask, *"Why* do we pray?" The only acceptable answer to that question is that we pray so that the Lord alone will be glorified. That desire is expressed in the first petition of the Lord's Prayer, "Hallowed be your name" (Matt. 6:9).

The first three requests in the Lord's Prayer focus on God and not on the people who are praying. The glorifying of God's name, the coming of God's kingdom, and the accomplishing of God's will on earth are the Lord's "prayer priorities" that we must prioritize as well. If we begin with these priorities and pray accordingly, then the way is open for the Father to answer us when we share our personal needs with him. "But seek first his kingdom and his righteousness, and all these things will be given to you as well" (Matt. 6:33). Among "these things" are daily bread, forgiveness of sins, and victory over temptations and trials (Matt. 6:11–13). If the provision of our personal needs doesn't in some way help to accomplish God's eternal purposes, then why should he answer our prayers?

Right motives are essential to a healthy Christian life. Other people see our actions and hear our words, but the Lord understands our motives and judges us accordingly (1 Cor. 4:5). *What* we do for him and *how* we do it are certainly important, but *why* we do it is also important. "People look at the outward appearance, but the LORD looks at the heart" (1 Sam. 16:7). Hypocrites pray only to be applauded for their piety, a practice that Jesus soundly condemned (Matt. 6:5; Luke 18:9–14).

One of my professors often said, "The purpose of preaching is to *express* and not to *impress*," and the same truth applies to our praying, especially our public praying. We should pray because we want the Father to be glorified, not because we want to impress him or anyone else with our vocabulary or our theology. How tragic to please everybody except God!

This first request in the Lord's Prayer makes it clear that prayer and worship go together. Too often we rush into God's presence, pour out our requests, and then rush back to our daily responsibilities, never pausing to worship him or even to thank him. David knew how to wed prayer with worship when he wrote, "May my prayer be set before you like incense; may the lifting up of my hands be like the evening sacrifice" (Ps. 141:2). He was referring to the two altars in the tabernacle: the brazen altar where the animals were sacrificed and the golden altar before the veil where the incense was burned each morning and evening. David probably wrote Psalm 141 while in the wilderness, far from the tabernacle; but this didn't keep him from worshiping his Lord. The lifting up of his hands represented the giving of himself to the Lord as a living sacrifice (Rom. 12:1), and his prayer was like fragrant incense rising to heaven; God accepted both. David was king, but here he saw himself as a priest, worshiping the Lord from his heart.

When we pray "hallowed be your name," we should pause to worship. We know that times of true worship give us better perspectives on the matters that concern us. The things that bother us don't seem quite as threatening when we quietly contemplate the greatness of our God and worship him. Children who speak to their parents only when they want something are selfish and forfeit a great deal of love, peace, and wisdom.

According to Numbers 13:26–33, ten of the twelve Hebrew spies who explored Canaan said they felt "like grasshoppers" when they saw the giants in the land. Had those ten men lifted their eyes of faith higher and beheld the greatness of the Lord, they would have seen that it was the giants who really were the grasshoppers! The unbelief of the ten spies discouraged the people, and as a result the nation wandered in the wilderness for thirty-eight years. Unbelief is always expensive. I've known individuals and ministries to suffer the same discipline because they would not obey the Lord and claim their spiritual inheritance by faith.

The Greek citizens in first-century Athens worshiped many false gods, including an idol inscribed "TO AN UNKNOWN GOD" (Acts 17:22–23). One of the Greek writers said that it was easier to find a god than a man in Athens, but at least the other deities had names. In his sermon to the members of the Areopagus, Paul identified this "unknown god" and told them about Jesus.

Names are important for identifying people, places, things, and events. The Lord gave names to the areas of his creation, such as *day* and *night*, *sky* and *land* (Gen. 1:5, 8, 10). Names involve not only identification but also authorization. Only those with authority have the right to give names or to change names. God gave Adam the authority to name the animals because Adam exercised dominion over creation (Gen. 1:27–30; 2:19–20; Psalm 8). It's important that God's children know their Father's name.

When God called Moses to return to Egypt and liberate his people, Moses wanted to know God's name just in case the people asked who had sent him. After all, who gave the fugitive Moses the right to tell the whole nation what to do? Moses had been off the scene for forty years! The Lord's answer was, "I AM WHO I AM" (Exod. 3:13–15). He also called himself "LORD" (note the capital letters), which is a translation of the Hebrew "Jehovah" or "Yahweh," from the three Hebrew letters rendered YHWH in English. Together they mean "to be" or "being" or "becoming." Jehovah is the personal, eternal, continuous, and absolute self-existent One, the living and true God, the I AM. The many names for God found in Scripture are derived from what he does—his mighty works—but Yahweh is derived from what he is, his person and personality, his glorious attributes.

The holy name Yahweh was spoken publicly only once a year on the Day of Atonement when the high priest blessed the people (Num. 6:22–27). Not wishing to violate the third commandment and perhaps incur judgment, the Jewish people refrained from using the sacred name Yahweh and substituted either *the Name* or *Adonai*—"the Lord" (not all capital letters). Among the Hebrew people, the phrase "his name" became a substitute for the holy name Jehovah.

For example, the tabernacle was the place where God dwelt and therefore where he put his name (Deut. 12:5). Those who spoke for God spoke in his name (Deut. 18:19–20). When the Jews praised God, they blessed his name (Ps. 96:2; 145:1) and made music to his name (Ps. 92:1). To pray was to call upon his name (Gen. 12:8; Ps. 79:6), and to love God was to love his name (Ps. 5:11). To extol his character was to "sing in praise of his name" (Ps. 68:4).

Christian believers know the Father because we know Jesus Christ the Son. Jesus said to the Father, "I have revealed you [Greek: 'your name'] to those whom you gave me out of the world" (John 17:6). The Jesus of the new covenant reveals the Jehovah of the old covenant. "I have made you known to them, and will continue to make you known in order that the love you have for me may be in them and that I myself may be in them" (John 17:26). Believers who allow the Holy Spirit to teach them from the Word will grow in their understanding of God's name and God's person.

Moses heard the name I AM WHO I AM, and when Jesus ministered here on earth, he literally "fleshed out" that name as recorded by the apostle John in his Gospel record. Jesus declared, "I am the bread of life" (6:35); "I am the light of the world" (8:12; 9:5); "I am the gate [KJV: door]" (10:9); "I am the good shepherd" (10:11); "I am the resurrection and the life" (11:25); "I am the way and the truth and the life" (14:6); and "I am the true vine" (15:1). Jesus is I AM WHO I AM and reveals the Father to us. The Savior becomes to us whatever spiritual blessing we need. God the Father revealed himself to Moses in a name; God the Son reveals that name to us in his person; and God the Holy Spirit reveals that person to us in our hearts from the Scriptures.

To Plato, God was "the idea of the good," and to Aristotle, "the Prime Mover." Hegel saw God as "the Absolute" and Herbert Spencer as "the Unknowable." Julian Huxley said that God was "a product of the human mind," and Sigmund Freud called God "an idealized superman." But to the family of faith, God is very real to us as the Father and the Son and the Holy Spirit. We pray in the name of Jesus and praise God in the name of Jesus. The Father has given to his Son "the name that is above every name, that at the name of Jesus every knee should bow, in heaven and on earth and under the earth, and every tongue acknowledge that Jesus Christ is Lord, to the glory of God the Father" (Phil. 2:9–11).

We are able to worship and pray because we know his name, but this is only the beginning.

The phrase "hallowed be your name" implies not only that we *know* God's name but also that we *reverence* God's name in every area of life. "So whether you eat or drink or whatever you do, do it all for the glory of God" (1 Cor. 10:31). In ancient Israel, blaspheming the holy name of God was a capital crime (Lev. 24:10–16). This included using his name in a profane manner and even violating legal oaths (Lev. 19:12). Unlike society today, how a person spoke about God was a serious matter in ancient days.

To hallow something means to set it apart as special, to dedicate it, to consecrate it to God for his special use. In the New Testament, it's a translation of the Greek word *hagiazo*, which is used in John 10:36 and 17:19 with reference to Jesus being "set apart" for his ministry. In John 17:17 it is applied to believers being set apart by the Word of God (see also Eph. 5:26). Abraham Lincoln used *hallow* in his famous Gettysburg Address: "In a larger sense we cannot dedicate, we cannot consecrate, we cannot hallow this ground." About the only familiar use of *hallow* today is found in the word *Halloween*, which is a contraction of "all hallows evening," the night before All Saints Day (October 31). It was once a sacred day on the church calendar, but in recent times an unbelieving society has made it quite something else.

"LORD, our Lord, how majestic is your name in all the earth!" wrote David in Psalm 8:1. Does anyone detect "majesty" in the average church service today, in our singing, praying, preaching, or public reading of the Scriptures? The eminent British theologian P. T. Forsyth tells of being in a meeting where a young man prayed, "O God, we have come to have a chat with Thee."[13] I've heard preachers refer to the Savior as "that guy Jesus" and to Moses as "this Moses character." Trivializing the precious treasures of the Christian faith is just the opposite of honoring God's majestic name, yet it goes on and grows worse.

God's name is not only majestic, it is also glorious. "Praise be to his glorious name forever; may the whole earth be filled with his glory" (Ps. 72:19). Is it God who is glorified in our assemblies or is it a great preacher or a great singer or a great choir? *Only God is great!* I love to hear a worship service opened with a biblical invocation instead of a folksy "Hi, folks! We're so glad you came!" Here's how the spiritual leaders in Nehemiah's day opened a service: "Blessed be your glorious name, and may it be exalted above all blessing and praise" (Neh. 9:5). Hearing those words, I feel like worshiping my Lord!

God can exalt his servants' names if he so chooses. There's nothing wrong with the servants of God being known widely for their faithful work for the Lord. God promised to make Abraham's name great (Gen. 12:2), and he said to David, "Now I will make your name great, like the names of the greatest men on earth" (2 Sam. 7:9, and see 8:13). Both Abraham and David had their faults, but in their heart of hearts they loved the Lord and sought to magnify his name. God magnified their names so that others might recognize that Jehovah was the true and living God. The Lord said to Joshua, "Today I will begin to exalt you in the eyes of all Israel, so they may know that I am with you as I was with Moses" (Josh. 3:7). Paul wrote about "the brother who is praised by all the churches for his service to the gospel" (2 Cor. 8:18), and he told the believers in Thessalonica to appreciate and love their faithful leaders (1 Thess. 5:12–13). There is nothing wrong with giving thanks to God's faithful servants, just as long as all the glory goes to God alone.

"Let them praise your great and awesome name," says Psalm 99:3. The Father gave to the Son "the name that is above every name" (Phil. 2:9), yet his exalted name is dragged into the sewers of filthy human speech day after day. Even well-meaning people carelessly use "minced oaths" to express themselves, words that are substitutes for the originals. They say "gee" or "jeez" instead of Jesus, "jiminy crickets" for Jesus Christ, "gosh" and "golly" for God, and on it goes. I saw a newspaper headline that read, "Lordy, Lordy, Now She's Forty," which is not only very poor poetry but terrible manners. The name of the Lord is great and awesome, as many people will discover when it's too late to change.

While we live in this world, one of our responsibilities is to magnify the name of the Lord. If we truly reverence Jesus in our hearts (1 Peter 3:15), we will ask God to use us to magnify him before an unbelieving world. "[L]et your light shine before others, that they may see your good deeds and glorify your Father in heaven" (Matt. 5:16). To most people, Jesus seems very far away, so we should be like telescopes that bring him closer so people can see him in us. Jesus seems very small and insignificant next to the media celebrities and sports heroes that people adore, but we should be like microscopes that make him larger and very important. We need to imitate Paul when he prayed "that now as always Christ will be exalted in my body, whether by life or by death" (Phil. 1:20). To magnify Jesus Christ and bring glory to him is our calling, no matter what our vocation might be.

Whatever the Lord does for his people, he does for the glory of his name:

Do we need his help and forgiveness? "Help us, God our Savior, for the glory of your name; deliver us and forgive our sins for your name's sake" (Ps. 79:9).

Do we need wisdom and direction? "He guides me along the right paths for his name's sake" (Ps. 23:3). "[F]or the sake of your name lead and guide me" (Ps. 31:3).

Are we seeking victory in one of life's battles? "May we shout for joy over your victory and lift up our banners in the name of our God" (Ps. 20:5). "All the nations surrounded me, but in the name of the LORD I cut them down" (Ps. 118:10).

Are we losing our hope? "And I will hope in your name, for your name is good" (Ps. 52:9).

The result of all this blessing is what Paul called "glory in the church and in Christ Jesus" (Eph. 3:21).

"For the sake of the name of the Lord" is a key to answered prayer. This is why we pray "in the name of Jesus," requesting what he would request and allowing the answer to glorify his name. As I've mentioned before, the purpose of prayer is not just to have God supply our needs but for God to be glorified in the answers that he sends.

We rob God of glory when we magnify ourselves and take the credit that rightly belongs to him. This is the mistake Moses made at Kadesh when in a fit of temper he struck the rock instead of speaking to it and said to the thirsty people, "Listen, you rebels, must we bring you water out of this rock?" (see Num. 20:1–13). God graciously sent the water, but he rebuked Moses for his pride and prohibited him from entering the Promised Land, even though Moses prayed that God would let him enter the land.

We rob God of glory when we profess one thing and practice another. "They claim to know God, but by their actions they deny him" (Titus 1:16). It was this sin that led to the destruction of Israel (the northern kingdom) and to the Babylonian captivity of Judah. "For my people have been taken away for nothing, and those who rule them mock. . . . And all day long my name is constantly blasphemed" (Isa. 52:5; see Rom. 2:24). The Babylonians taunted the Jews and said, "Sing us one of the songs of Zion" (Ps. 137:3), but the captives had lost their song and were unable to magnify the Lord. The prophet Ezekiel, living with the exiles in Babylon, told them that their captivity was for the sake of honoring God's holy name, which they had "profaned among the nations" (Ezek. 36:22–23). Israel claimed to worship the true and living God, yet the nation was in bondage to pagan idol worshipers!

The nation of Israel was privileged to have special blessings from the Lord that no other nation possessed. Foremost among these blessings was the presence of God's glory in their midst (Rom. 9:1–5). The cloud of God's glory hovered above the tabernacle, and when the nation marched the cloud guided them through the wilderness (Exod. 40:34–38). God's glory also dwelt in the temple (1 Kings 8:10–11), but the rulers and the people so defiled the temple with their wickedness that the glory moved out (Ezek. 9:3; 10:4, 18; 11:23). Over the great city of Jerusalem, Israel could write the name *Ichabod*, meaning "the Glory has departed" (1 Sam. 4:21–22).

Has the glory of God departed from some of our homes, churches, and parachurch ministries *and we don't realize it?* Is there really "glory in the church" or just crowds of people seeking religious entertainment? Not to desire to glorify God is the beginning of sin and leads to a dark and foolish heart (Rom. 1:21). God in his longsuffering gave his people many years to awaken to their need and forsake their sins, but they refused to listen. Are we imitating their bad example?

Magnifying the name of the Lord is one of the major themes of the prophet Malachi. The Jewish priests showed contempt for God's name by routinely going through the motions of ministry but keeping the best for themselves (Malachi 1). They had no fear of the Lord and were dishonoring him among the Gentile nations. The priests were unfaithful to their privileged calling and had turned away from the Word of God (2:1–9). The people had broken God's covenant and refused to bring their tithes to God's house, so the Lord held back the rain (3:6–12). However, there was a faithful remnant in the land, people who revered God's name and prayed, and the Lord heard their prayers and blessed them (3:16–4:6).

Are we today a part of God's faithful praying remnant, or are we among the bored believers who give God second best and can hardly wait for the church service to end so we can be early at the restaurant or the golf course? The prophet Malachi asked the careless priests and worshipers, "When you sacrifice lame or diseased animals, is that not wrong? Try offering them to your governor! Would he be pleased with you?" (Mal. 1:8). Do we prepare to worship the Lord with the same care we would exercise if we had an appointment with the governor or the president of the United States? Do ministers prepare their messages knowing that the Lord is the most important listener? Or are we just "getting by" in our service to the Lord? Are we satisfied with religious mediocrity?

When I see worshipers arriving late and walking into the sanctuary carrying cups of coffee, I wonder if they would arrive late to see the president at the White House and carry their cups into the Oval Office. We try to arrive at the doctor's office early, even though we may have to wait, but it's convenient to arrive at church late and make a grand entrance. I recall visiting a famous national historical site, and the sign at the door read: "No Smoking—No Food—No Chewing Gum." I wanted to get copies for the church I was serving. Standing on a church platform, I've often seen people in the congregation chewing gum one minute and singing "Holy, Holy, Holy" the next minute.

There is a better way for those who revere God's name (Mal. 4:2).

God's name is glorified when God's people know his name, reverence his name, and magnify his name before an unbelieving world by trusting him to accomplish his work in them and through them. "But you will receive power when the Holy Spirit comes on you; and you will be my witnesses in Jerusalem, and in all Judea and Samaria, and to the ends of the earth" (Acts 1:8). Before those early believers went out to serve, they waited and prayed for ten days behind closed doors. But when the Spirit came upon them, they opened the doors and went out to evangelize the Roman Empire.

Many different names are recorded in the book of Acts, but the most important name is the name of Jesus Christ. *It is the name of Jesus Christ that is the secret of success in the Christian life and in the ministry of the Christian church.* God's people gather together to worship, not in the name of a denomination, a preacher, or even the church, but in the name of Jesus (Matt. 18:20). God's people pray in the name of Jesus (John 14:13–14; 15:6; 16:23–26) and declare boldly that Jesus is the *only* Savior (Acts 2:21; 4:12). The world at large doesn't appreciate or accept this message, so God's people suffer for the name of Jesus and thank God for the privilege (Matt. 10:22; John 15:18–25; Acts 5:40–42). Or do we?

I'm not suggesting that effective ministry requires us to perform signs and wonders as the apostles did, because people who perform apostolic miracles must have apostolic gifts. I am saying that the effective ministry of the early church was because they had faith in the name of Jesus. They prayed in that name (Acts 4:23–31), preached that name (4:12–18), and were willing to suffer for that name (5:41). The power of his name is released by the faith of his people, and this power can bring forgiveness (Acts 2:38; 4:12; 10:43), healing (3:6–10; 4:8–12), deliverance (16:18), and boldness (4:29–30). The world doesn't care if we use words like *God* or *Lord*, but if we use the name *Jesus* we declare war. Not to speak the name of Jesus is to announce our defeat and abandon the very purpose for which God left us on this planet. We cannot pray "hallowed be your name" unless the lives we live and the work we do depend on the power of Jesus's name.

The religious leaders in Jerusalem commanded the apostles to stop preaching in the name of Jesus because they had filled Jerusalem with his name (Acts 4:18–22; 5:27–28). But the believers persisted in their witness. We certainly cannot be silent about such an exalted name as the name of Jesus, "the name that is above every name." People who today shake their fists at the mention of his name will one day bow their knees and confess that Jesus is Lord (Phil. 2:9–11). Yes, the name of Jesus is an exclusive name, because he claims to be the Son of God and the only Savior—and he is! Peter said it clearly: "Salvation is found in no one else, for there is no other name given under heaven by which we must be saved" (Acts 4:12).

"Some trust in chariots and some in horses, but we trust in the name of the LORD our God" (Ps. 20:7). If you want a twenty-first-century application of that verse, I suggest: "Some trust in money and management, others in clever promotion and sophisticated equipment, and some in Hollywood-style religious entertainment, but we will give ourselves to prayer and God's Word and trust in the name of Jesus." I'm not suggesting that we abandon the use of excellent ministry equipment, only that the people who handle the equipment know how to pray and trust God to use them to be a blessing. "Those who know your name trust in you, for you, LORD, have never forsaken those who seek you" (Ps. 9:10).

While rereading the book of Revelation, I was struck by the number of times John uses the word *name*—thirty-eight to be exact. John describes the contrasts and conflicts between heaven and earth, Jerusalem and Babylon, the bride of Christ and the harlot, Christ and the antichrist, the Lamb and the beast. The saints he describes are true to Christ's name and willing to endure hardship rather than deny his name (2:3, 13; 3:8). They revere his name in spite of the opposition of Satan and his demons (11:18). The beast slanders God's name (13:5–7) and insists that everybody obey him and wear his mark (13:11–17). The world worships and serves the antichrist, but the saints worship and serve Christ and honor his name (15:3–4).

It costs something to be identified with the name of Jesus Christ, but when you consider the end of the story, you see that the blessings are worth the price: "They will see his face, and his name will be on their foreheads" (Rev. 20:4).

If we anticipate wearing his name in the future, let's glorify his name today; and when we pray "hallowed be your name," let's really mean it.

Holy God, We Praise Thy Name

Holy God, we praise Thy name;
Lord of all, we bow before Thee;
All on earth Thy scepter claim,
All in heav'n above adore Thee.
Infinite Thy vast domain,
Everlasting is Thy reign.

Hark, the loud celestial hymn
Angel choirs above are raising;
Cherubim and Seraphim
In unceasing chorus praising,
Fill the heav'ns with sweet accord:
Holy, holy, holy Lord.

Lo! The apostolic train
Joins Thy sacred name to hallow;
Prophets swell the glad refrain,
And the white-robed martyrs follow;
And from morn to set of sun,
Through the Church the song goes on.

Holy Father, Holy Son,
Holy Spirit, Three we name Thee;
While in essence only One,
Undivided God we claim Thee,
And adoring bend the knee,
While we sing our praise to Thee.

4th Century *Te Deum*
Translated by Clarence Walworth

Citizenship

"Your kingdom come"

It was a sad day in the history of Israel when the elders fired the godly prophet and prayer warrior Samuel and asked God to give them "a king to lead us, such as all the other nations have" (1 Sam. 8:5).

It should have been the other way around. Israel was appointed to be "a people who live apart" (Num. 23:9), and the Gentile nations should have been begging Israel to share with them the truth about their great God, Jehovah. The neighboring nations had sanctuaries, but only Israel had the glorious presence of God dwelling in their tabernacle. The nations had laws, but Israel's law had been handed down from heaven. Israel's neighbors prayed to man-made gods who were powerless to help, but the God of Israel is the living God who heard his people's prayers and answered them.

According to Judges 1–2, Israel was a bad example and a poor witness to its neighbors, so we shouldn't be surprised to see Israel imitating the pagan nations and begging for a king. Since the days of Abraham, the true and living God had been their king, and now the elders wanted to replace Jehovah with a weak, fallible human being. "Listen to all that the people are saying to you," the Lord said to Samuel; "it is not you they have rejected, but they have rejected me as their king" (1 Sam. 8:7). This was the first of three rejections in Israel's history that ultimately brought about their worldwide dispersion and the destruction of their temple; but more about that later.

The Lord wanted Israel to be "a kingdom of priests and a holy nation" (Exod. 19:6), but they disobeyed him and became more and more like the nations around them. Today, the church has the calling of being "a chosen people, a royal priesthood, a holy nation, God's special possession" (1 Peter 2:9), but are we living up to this privilege? It seems to me that the church is more and more conforming to the world instead of converting the world. Like ancient Israel, we want our leaders to do what we want and not what God wants.

🛐🛐🛐🛐🛐

When we pray "your kingdom come," we affirm that God is King. "For the LORD Most High is awesome, the great King over all the earth" (Ps. 47:2). "The LORD reigns, let the earth be glad; let the distant shores rejoice" (Ps. 97:1). "The LORD reigns, let the nations tremble; he sits enthroned between the cherubim, let the earth shake" (Ps. 99:1). "I will exalt you, my God the King; I will praise your name for ever and ever" (Ps. 145:1). Jesus Christ is "the ruler of the kings of the earth" (Rev. 1:5) and "Lord of lords and King of kings" (Rev. 17:14; see 1 Tim. 6:15 and Rev. 19:16).

We who have trusted Jesus Christ are not only citizens of God's kingdom but also children of the King. "Blessed are the poor in spirit, for theirs is the kingdom of heaven. . . . Blessed are the peacemakers, for they will be called children of God" (Matt. 5:3, 9). When I was confirmed, our confirmation hymn was "A Child of the King," and the song has come to my mind often during these many years of ministry. The third verse reads:

> I once was an outcast stranger on earth,
> A sinner by choice and an alien by birth;

But I've been adopted, my name's written down,
An heir to a mansion, a robe, and a crown.
I'm a child of the King, a child of the King:
With Jesus my Savior, I'm a child of the King.

Harriet E. Buell

That may not be great poetry, but it certainly is encouraging theology. Our prayers are not in vain, for God's kingdom *is* going to come. "The kingdom of the world has become the kingdom of the Lord and of his Messiah, and he will reign for ever and ever" (Rev. 11:15). Jesus said to his disciples, "Do not be afraid, little flock, for your Father has been pleased to give you the kingdom" (Luke 12:32). The Father doesn't just give us a kingdom ID card or a kingdom address. *He gives us the kingdom!*

What kind of kingdom is it?

⚜⚜⚜⚜⚜

"My kingdom is not of this world," Jesus told the Roman governor Pilate. "If it were, my servants would fight to prevent my arrest by the Jewish leaders. But now my kingdom is from another place" (John 18:36). Pilate was a Roman official, and when he heard the word *kingdom* he thought in terms of authority, force, armies, and battles. But our Lord's kingdom doesn't follow the Roman pattern. Our example is Jesus Christ, not Julius Caesar.

"You know that those who are regarded as rulers of the Gentiles lord it over them," Jesus taught the Twelve, "and their high officials exercise authority over them. Not so with you. Instead, whoever wants to become great among you must be your servant, and whoever wants to be first must be slave of all. For even the Son of Man did not come to be served, but to serve, and to give his life as a ransom for many" (Mark 10:42–45).

Jesus told a confused Nicodemus that the only way to enter this kingdom of heaven was by believing on him and being born again (John 3:1–18). Because sin is reigning (Rom. 5:21), death is reigning (Rom. 5:14, 17); but because Christ is reigning in heaven, grace is reigning (Rom. 5:21) *and spiritually dead sinners can be born again with new life!*

Jesus was born a king (Matt. 2:2). The angels praised him and a royal star guided the magi who came from afar to pay homage to the King of the Jews (Matt. 2:1–12).

Jesus lived like a true king, not in pomp and splendor but in humility and poverty, for "the kingdom of God is not a matter of eating and drinking, but of righteousness, peace and joy in the Holy Spirit" (Rom. 14:17). "He seemed to be doing nothing," wrote G. Campbell Morgan. "He was gathering no army. He was making no proclamations. He was calling together no parliament of men. He was simply walking about, healing a few, speaking to individuals and companies of men."[14] How unlike the kingdom makers today!

Jesus displayed his kingship over wind and waves, schools of fish, physical diseases and deformities, and even demons. When he called men to follow him and serve God, they obeyed, even though they must have felt frightened and inadequate. The kingdom laws that he enunciated focused on love, humility, sacrifice, and forgiveness. His message was filled with paradoxes: the way to rise higher is to go lower; the way to lead is to serve; the way to receive is to give; the way to succeed is to seem to fail. Unlike many leaders, he practiced what he preached and brought glory to the Father.

He died a king, in full control of the situation. The soldiers crowned him with thorns and decked him in a mock coronation robe, bowing before him, anointing him with their spittle, and saying, "Hail, king of the Jews!" (Matt. 27:27–31). The indictment displayed over his head on the cross was "THIS IS JESUS, THE KING OF THE JEWS" (Matt. 27:37). Death did not take him; he willed his own death and in that death defeated death forever. By the grace of God, Jesus tasted death for everyone (Heb. 2:9).

Jesus proved his kingly victory by his resurrection from the dead, "because it was impossible for death to keep its hold upon him" (Acts 2:24). He ascended to heaven, the victorious King, and today is enthroned at the right hand of the Father (Acts 2:33–35). Today he is a priest "in the order of Melchizedek." *Melchizedek* means "king of righteousness," so Jesus is ministering to his church today as both King and Priest (Ps. 110:4; Heb. 6:20–7:10).

> Lifted up was He to die,
> "It is finished," was His cry;
> Now in heaven exalted high,
> Hallelujah! What a Savior!
>
> P. P. Bliss

One day Christ will return as King of Kings and Lord of Lords (Rev. 19:11–21). He will defeat the enemies of truth and righteousness and usher in "a new heaven and a new earth, where righteousness dwells" (2 Peter 3:13). In that wonderful new world, "his servants will serve him" and "they will reign for ever and ever" (Rev. 22:3, 5).

If Jesus is the victorious King, why is this world so fragmented and fearful? And why is the church in such disarray and seeming defeat? For the same reason that ancient Israel was divided and defeated: they rejected their heavenly King and asked for an earthly king so they could imitate the godless nations. Instead of rejoicing that they were God's unique and special people, they imitated the pagan nations and sacrificed their distinctive witness.

One mistake often leads to another. Israel rejected God the Father when they fired Samuel. Then Jesus came to earth and Israel rejected God the Son, demanding that he be crucified. "We have no king but Caesar," the chief priests answered Pilate (John 19:15). The Holy Spirit came upon the church at Pentecost (Acts 2) and through the apostles and other believers brought salvation to thousands of people. But Israel's religious leaders rejected the witness of the Holy Spirit, culminating in the stoning of Stephen (Acts 7:54–60). Stephen said as he concluded his message, "You are just like your ancestors: You always resist the Holy Spirit" (Acts 7:51).

Israel's rejections meant the loss of their God, for the leaders had rejected the Father, the Son, and the Holy Spirit! The Lord did not reject his people (Rom. 10:21), but he turned from Israel to the Gentiles (Acts 10), fulfilling the words of Jesus, "Therefore I tell you that the kingdom of God will be taken away from you and given to a people who will produce its fruit" (Matt. 21:43). That "people" is the church, "a chosen people, a royal priesthood, a holy nation, God's special possession, that you may declare the praises of him who called you out of darkness into his wonderful light" (1 Peter 2:9).

Christians are a special people called to accomplish the special task of making Christ known throughout this dark and doomed world. The word translated "declare" in 1 Peter 2:9 means "to proclaim, to advertise." Our task as a chosen people is to advertise by our words and deeds the glorious virtues of Jesus Christ. We are to live and serve in such a way that others will want what we have in Jesus Christ.

But how can the church advertise the virtues of Christ *if the church is imitating the world*? We have been called to shine as lights, not to reflect as mirrors. We don't belong to this world system (John 17:14–19) but to a heavenly counterculture that is hated by the same world system that hated Jesus and crucified him. This spiritual kingdom did not originate from the world nor is it sustained by the world (John 18:36–37). If we pray "your kingdom come" while at the same time compromising with the world, we are hypocrites and our prayers will not be answered.

If we sincerely pray "your kingdom come," there are some conditions to meet. Our lives must be different from the lives of the lost people and the careless Christians around us. People who really want Jesus to come and who look forward to his glorious kingdom will be guided by Paul's first letter to the Thessalonian church. Each chapter in this letter ends with a reference to the coming of Jesus Christ and tells us how we should live if we are sincerely looking for his coming.

The Thessalonian believers "turned to God from idols to serve the living and true God, and to wait for his Son from heaven, whom he raised from the dead—Jesus, who rescues us from the coming wrath" (1 Thess. 1:9–10). We are worshiping and serving either the true and living God in heaven or the idols of this world. When these people turned *to* God, they also turned *away from* the useless idols they had worshiped, because they knew that no one can serve two masters (Matt. 6:24). How subtle is "Christian idol-worship" as we boast of our buildings, our finances, our accomplishments, and our statistics, instead of boasting in the Lord.

First Thessalonians chapter 2 ends with a description of the joy Paul anticipated when he would see his friends in heaven. "For what is our hope, our joy, or the crown in which we will glory in the presence of the Lord Jesus when he comes? Is it not you? Indeed, you are our glory and joy" (2:19–20). Christians who want Jesus to come back are faithful witnesses who seek to reach others with the gospel. What a tragedy it would be to go to heaven and have no one to greet you!

At the end of chapter 3, the emphasis is on *love and holiness* (vv. 11–13). If we don't love others and live godly lives, why would we want Jesus to come back and find us in a state of disobedience? Our Lord's parable of the unfaithful servant (Matt. 24:45–51) tells us what happens to believers who mentally postpone Christ's coming and begin to abuse people and neglect their ministries. How can we long for his appearing (2 Tim. 4:8) if we don't walk in the light and walk in love?

Encouragement is the theme of the closing verses of 1 Thessalonians 4. The believers in Thessalonica were not having an easy time of it: the church was being persecuted and some of the believers had died. Paul assured them that when Jesus returned, their suffering would be turned to glorious joy and they would be reunited with their loved ones. *This is the greatest comfort we have in the midst of suffering and sorrow.* We must not see our Lord's return as an escape from burdens and battles but as an encouragement to keep on working and warring *because it is worth it!*

Paul's closing words in chapter 5 admonish us to live sanctified lives that are separated from sin and surrendered to the Lord (5:23–24). "All who have this hope in him [Christ] purify themselves, just as he is pure" (1 John 3:3). A man and woman engaged to be married will keep themselves pure, and the church that anticipates being married to Jesus the Bridegroom will stay pure in preparation for that heavenly wedding (Rev. 19:6–9).

Praying "your kingdom come" involves more than simply uttering three words. *It demands the devotion and dedication of our entire being to Jesus as we eagerly anticipate seeing him!* Heaven is not simply a destination; it is a motivation. Because of the cross, all born-again Christians are ready to go to heaven (John 14:1–6), but not all are prepared for the judgment seat of Christ where "we will all give an account of ourselves to God" (Rom. 14:12). "For we must all appear before the judgment seat of Christ, that everyone may receive what is due them for the things done while in the body, whether good or bad" (2 Cor. 5:10).

The next time we pray "your kingdom come" we need to review our own lives and ask whether we would really be happy if Jesus came back today, or if we want him to come only to end our problems.

Near the end of *Fiddler on the Roof* is a brief but poignant conversation that may help us better understand the use and abuse of a future hope.

The Russian authorities gave the residents of the Jewish village of Anatevka three days to clear out and find other places to live. Mendel, son of the rabbi, says to his father, "Rabbi, we've been waiting for the Messiah all our lives. Wouldn't this be a good time for him to come?"

His father replies, "We'll have to wait for him someplace else. Meanwhile, let's start packing."

Like some people today, Mendel saw the coming of Messiah only as the perfect solution to the painful problems of life. Let Messiah come! In an instant, the enemy will be defeated and the village will be rescued! But the beloved rabbi had the correct approach. To paraphrase his reply: "The promise doesn't change, only our location changes, and we can take the promise with us. The promise must not be an excuse for indolence. Now, get to work!"

During the three years of our Lord's ministry on earth, many people expected him to break the Roman yoke and establish the kingdom for Israel. When Jesus rode into Jerusalem on what we call Palm Sunday, some of the people shouted, "Blessed is the coming kingdom of our father David" (Mark 11:10). He told the crowd the parable of the pounds [minas] "because he was near Jerusalem and the people thought that the kingdom of God was going to appear at once" (Luke 19:11). After his resurrection, even the apostles asked him, "Lord, are you at this time going to restore the kingdom to Israel?" (Acts 1:6). Jesus didn't deny the fact of the future kingdom; he merely told them they had other things to do first.

Yes, Jesus will one day reign in his glorious kingdom (Matt. 20:20–28; Rev. 20:4–6), but until then he reigns in and through "those who receive God's abundant provision of grace and of the gift of righteousness [who] reign in life through the one man, Jesus Christ" (Rom. 5:17). The kingdom of God on earth is wherever the Son of God is loved and worshiped and God the Father is glorified through obedience to his will. The gospel is "the good news of the kingdom of God and the name of Jesus Christ" (Acts 8:12). The second and third requests in the Lord's Prayer go together: "your kingdom come, your will be done on earth as it is in heaven."

Church history records the embarrassment of religious people who were sure they knew exactly when the Lord would return, only to be proven wrong. This kind of prophetic presumption started back in Paul's day, as recorded in 2 Thessalonians. Somebody brought a forged letter to the assembly in Thessalonica, claiming it was from Paul. It asserted that the day of the Lord had come and that the return of Jesus would shortly occur. Some of the saints believed this lie and quit their jobs to get ready to meet their soon-coming Savior. But this meant they had to be fed by the believers who were still faithfully working for a living.

In his letter, Paul untangled their theological confusion and then admonished the idle believers to get back to work. Jesus made it clear that his followers should be working while they are watching and waiting, for this is the best preparation for meeting the Lord at his return (see Matt. 24:42–25:30; Mark 13:32–37; Luke 12:35–48). "What I say to you, I say to everyone: 'Watch!' " (Mark 13:37). This is balanced by, "Anyone who is unwilling to work shall not eat" (2 Thess. 3:10). No matter where we live on this earth, we have the promise of the Lord's coming. But we also have the responsibility of obeying God's will and "making the most of every opportunity, because the days are evil" (Eph. 5:16).

※※※※※

Assuming that our character, conduct, and motives are pleasing to the Lord, does the Lord's Prayer give us the right to ask the Father to send Jesus sooner? Is it possible that our humble prayers will help to determine when the Lord will return? Such an idea sounds preposterous, yet Jesus tells us to pray that his kingdom will come.

In 1 Corinthians 16:22, Paul prayed that Jesus might return. "If anyone does not love the Lord, let that person be cursed [*anathema*]! Come, Lord [*marana tha*]!" The Aramaic phrase *marana tha* can mean "our Lord, come" or "our Lord comes." Some students think that *marana tha* was used by the early church at the close of the Lord's Supper to express their confidence in the coming of the Lord, and perhaps both meanings were intended. "Our Lord is coming! Our Lord, come!"

In Revelation 22:20, the apostle John responded to Christ's statement "Yes, I am coming soon" by saying, "Amen. Come, Lord Jesus." Once again, this can be a confession of faith or an expression of loving desire, a prayer for Jesus to return.

But the key text is 2 Peter 3:9–12.

The Lord is not slow in keeping his promise, as some understand slowness. Instead he is patient with you, not wanting anyone to perish, but everyone to come to repentance. But the day of the Lord will come like a thief. The heavens will disappear with a roar; the elements will be destroyed by fire, and the earth and everything done in it will be laid bare. Since everything will be destroyed in this way, what kind of people ought you to be? You ought to live holy and godly lives as you look forward to the day of God and speed its coming.

That last phrase, "speed its coming," is variously translated as "earnestly desiring" (ASV), "expecting and helping to hasten the coming" (Weymouth), "looking for and hastening the coming" (NASB), and "awaiting and hastening the coming" (Williams).

Peter seems to be telling the believers ("you" in 3:1, 9, 11) that the Lord is patient with them, for they ought to be sharing the gospel and winning the lost. The Lord will one day judge the world and usher in "the day of God" (v. 12). By living godly lives and winning the lost, Christians will "help to hasten" the coming of the new heaven and new earth. God isn't slow in keeping his promises. It's the church that is slow in praying and in getting the message out to a lost world. Revelation 5:8 and 8:3–4 indicate that the prayers of God's people are not lost or forgotten but are preserved in heaven, eventually to be answered. Why couldn't this include "your kingdom come"?

When we trusted Jesus as Savior and Lord, the Father "rescued us from the dominion [authority] of darkness and brought us into the kingdom of the Son he loves" (Col. 1:13). The Greek word translated "brought into" pictures prisoners of war being liberated and transferred to the place where they belong. We are citizens of the kingdom of God (Phil. 3:20) and have all the rights and privileges of that citizenship, including life, liberty, and love. We have also been rescued "from the present evil age" (Gal. 1:4) and will be rescued "from the coming wrath" at the return of Jesus Christ (1 Thess. 1:10). "So if the Son sets you free, you will be free indeed" (John 8:36).

Since we are privileged to be citizens in God's kingdom right now, we must abandon our own "kingdoms" and make God's kingdom the only one we honor and serve. To limp between the kingdom of God and the kingdom of this world is to miss the best of both, according to Matthew 6:33. Years ago, we used to sing a chorus that expressed it perfectly. I think Al Smith wrote it.

> With eternity's values in view, Lord,
> With eternity's values in view,
> Let me do each day's work for Jesus,
> With eternity's values in view.

This means, of course, living in the future tense and not being shackled by the past or pressured by the present. It means living in obedience to the wisdom of God and not depending on the wisdom of this world (1 Cor. 1:18–31). God's wisdom is like gold, silver, and costly stones, materials that will endure the fire of God's judgment; but the cleverness of this world system is like wood, hay, or straw, materials that will burn to ashes (1 Cor. 3:10–23).

G. Campbell Morgan wrote, "Therefore a man must be prepared to do violence to all his own wit and wisdom and cleverness, and be assured that the method of preaching the Gospel to the poor, and healing the sick, and opening blind eyes, and refusing to gather an army, and failing to call together a parliament, are the real methods of the kingdom."[15] Imagine his disappointment if he could see the way some churches are promoted today and how many "parliaments" pastors call in hopes of discovering some clever new idea.

"Your kingdom come" implies that God rules first of all in our lives and then through us in the lives of others as we pray for them and minister to them. We want God's kingdom to rule in homes and families, in places of employment and ministry, in various government offices and agencies, and in places of authority and ministry around the world. Until Jesus comes again and establishes the kingdom of glory, we can pray that his kingdom of grace will have great influence through his church.

Someone has said, "The secret of happiness is to have someone to love, something to do, and something to look forward to." Certainly we who have trusted Jesus have someone to love, and he asks us as he asked Peter, "Simon son of John, do you love me more than these?" (see John 21:15–19). Jesus didn't ask Peter about his doctrine or his progress in preaching. He asked Peter if he loved him most of all. That's the foundation for ministry and the first step toward happiness.

As for the "something to do," I can't conceive of a Christian believer with nothing to do! Once you discover your spiritual giftedness, you want to use those abilities for the glory of God and the building of the church. The joy of serving Jesus cannot be duplicated by the world.

We have something to look forward to, because Jesus is coming again. "Your kingdom come" is a prayer that he will answer; and as we wait and watch, praying that prayer will keep us awake and alert.

Someone to love means worshiping.

Something to do means working and witnessing.

Something to look forward to means waiting and watching.

"But our citizenship is in heaven. And we eagerly await a Savior from there, the Lord Jesus Christ" (Phil. 3:20).

"Your kingdom come."

Lo! He Comes, with Clouds Descending

Lo! He comes, with clouds descending,
Once for favored sinners slain;
Thousand, thousand saints attending
Swell the triumph of His train;
Hallelujah! Hallelujah! Hallelujah!
God appears on earth to reign,
God appears on earth to reign.

Every eye shall now behold Him,
Robed in dreadful majesty;
Those who set at naught and sold Him,
Pierced and nailed Him to the tree,
Deeply wailing, deeply wailing, deeply wailing,
Shall the true Messiah see,
Shall the true Messiah see.

The dear tokens of His passion
Still His dazzling body bears;
Cause of endless exultation
To His ransomed worshipers;
With what rapture, with what rapture, with what
      rapture,
Gaze we on those glorious scars!
Gaze we on those glorious scars!

Yea, Amen! Let all adore Thee,
High on Thy eternal throne;
Savior, take the power and glory,
Claim the kingdom for Thine own;
Hallelujah! Hallelujah! Hallelujah!
Everlasting God, come down!
Everlasting God, come down!

Charles Wesley

Partnership

"Your will be done, on earth as it is in heaven"

There was a time when heaven and earth existed in perfect harmony and God could survey his creation and call it "very good" (Gen. 1:31). Indeed, in the beginning everything in creation was working in beautiful harmony because only one will was operating in the universe, and that was the perfect will of God. However, the rebellion of Lucifer (Isa. 14:12–15) and the disobedience of our first parents (Genesis 3; Rom. 5:12–21) introduced other wills into the world, and this brought division and conflict between heaven and earth. In heaven, God's will is always done by the angels and the saints in glory; but on earth, lost sinners, demons, and even God's own people rebel against the Lord and want to have their own way.

God in his grace seeks to bring heaven and earth together, and he will never change his plan. He bridged the gulf between heaven and earth by sending three gifts to our rebellious planet: his inspired Word, his beloved Son, and the Holy Spirit. The Holy Spirit reveals the Son of God to us as we read the Word of God, and those who trust Jesus are born into the family of God and have the privilege of speaking to God in prayer. *Prayer is a "partnership" between God and his church that enables him to accomplish his will on earth*

77

through the witness of his obedient people. The apostolic church put "prayer and the ministry of the word" first on their agenda (Acts 6:4), and so should the church today.

The immediate purpose of prayer is the accomplishing of God's will on earth; the ultimate purpose of prayer is the eternal glory of God. This is why Robert Law wrote, "Prayer is a mighty instrument, not for getting man's will done in heaven, but for getting God's will done on earth."[16] True prayer means more than simply asking for what we think we need and adding Jesus's name to the list; it means praying as Jesus prayed. "My Father, if it is possible, let this cup be taken from me. Yet not as I will, but as you will" (Matt. 26:39). Our Lord's half-brother James understood this distinction and wrote, "When you ask, you do not receive, because you ask with wrong motives, that you may spend what you get on your pleasures" (James 4:3).

Again, consider Robert Law's words above: "Prayer is a mighty instrument, not for getting man's will done in heaven, but for getting God's will done on earth." *The believers praying on earth must be available for God to use them to help answer their prayers if that is his will.* True prayer is a partnership between heaven and earth. The apostle Paul understood this important truth and frequently requested the churches to pray that God would accomplish his will in and through him.[17] Even with all of his education, spiritual insight, and experience, Paul knew that he could not do his work alone.

Before sin entered the human race, our first parents were in partnership with God and doing his will. God created the animals, but it was Adam who gave them their names (Gen. 2:18–20). God planted a garden for Adam and Eve to live in, but they had to tend it (Gen. 2:8–15). In the conception of their children, the man and woman shared the creative work of God, in whose image they had been made. Before sin entered the world, what was done on earth was willed from heaven and given heaven's blessing. There was no fear in the human heart, nor was there any desire to try to change God's mind. It was pure partnership between a loving God and our first parents who loved their Creator. It was not until sin entered the scene that the man and woman hid from God.

Occasionally I have counseled with people who were actually afraid of the will of God and terrified at the thought of surrendering themselves completely to him. Even familiar verses like Romans 12:1–2 disturbed them because they had concluded that the will of God was something painful and perilous that must be avoided. They were sure that if they yielded themselves to Christ, they would be sent to some distant and dangerous place where they would waste away in oblivion. There would be no joys, no adventures, no love or marriage; just loneliness and a monochrome miserable existence.

In our conversation, I would have them read Psalm 33:11 aloud several times—"But the plans of the LORD stand firm forever, the purposes of his heart through all generations." Once they grasped the beautiful truth that *the will of God comes from the heart of God*, their fears began to fade away. They had to understand that what God wills for his children is the expression of his love for them. "Perfect love drives out fear" (1 John 4:18).

If they still needed more encouragement, I would show them John 4:34 where Jesus says, "My food . . . is to do the will of him who sent me and to finish his work." *The will of God is nourishment, not punishment!* To live and serve in the will of God means to mature spiritually day after day, to discover our gifts and use them joyfully, and to become all that we can become for the glory of God. The more we do the Lord's will, the more we enjoy the Lord's best blessings *that he has tailor-made especially for us.* When it comes to God's will, one size does not fit all. God's plan for each of his children is individual and personal.

Listen again to Robert Law: "God is Love. The Will of God is pure, unchangeable, holy Love working for the highest goal of every creature."[18] Partnership with the Lord in prayer and service is a deepening expression of his divine love for us and our love for him, for his people, and for a lost world. Can we want anything greater than this?

God's will is not only the expression of his love and the imparting of spiritual nourishment, but it's the sharing of Christ's yoke. "Come to me, all you who are weary and burdened, and I will give you rest. Take my yoke upon you and learn from me, for I am gentle and humble in heart, and you will find rest for your souls. For my yoke is easy and my burden is light" (Matt. 11:28–30).

Those words are so familiar that it's easy to miss the full message they convey. Christ was addressing people who were weary from struggling against the cares of life, and who were burdened by the demands of a difficult religious system that didn't come from the Lord (Matthew 23). Our Lord gave three invitations: *come, take,* and *learn.* If they *came* to him, he would give them rest in their hearts because their sins would be forgiven. If they *took his yoke,* he would walk with them and help them carry their burdens. And if they *learned from him,* they would find a deeper rest in his grace and love.

The unconverted person wears a heavy yoke of sin that grows heavier each day. The outwardly religious person wears a yoke of rules and rituals that bring no relief. But the children of God are united to Christ and wear a yoke that is easy ("fitted"). They carry a burden that is light, because "his commands are not burdensome" (1 John 5:3). This is a summary of true discipleship.

When we pray for God's will to be done in our lives and in God's world, we are walking in the light (see 1 John 1:5–10). God's Word is a lamp (Ps. 119:105), and "the unfolding of [his] words gives light; it gives understanding to the simple"

80

(Ps. 119:130). "For this command is a lamp, this teaching is a light" (Prov. 6:23). "The path of the righteous is like the morning sun, shining ever brighter till the full light of day" (Prov. 4:18).

As we walk in the light, God gives us more light. The account of Paul's conversion illustrates this truth. It is given three times in the book of Acts. In Acts 9:3 Luke tells us that "a light from heaven flashed around him [Paul]." Looking back on that experience, Paul himself says, "A bright light from heaven flashed around me" (Acts 22:6). Later Paul told King Agrippa, "I saw a light from heaven, brighter than the sun" (Acts 26:13). "A light . . . a bright light . . . a light brighter than the sun. . . ." In Paul's spiritual walk, the light kept shining brighter, and so it should be in our walk with the Lord.

Jesus compared doing God's will to drinking the cup the Father prepared for him (John 18:10–11; Mark 14:32–36). Peter wanted to protect Jesus from arrest and trial, but it was the Father's will that the Son suffer and die. If the Father has "mixed" the contents of the cup especially for us, should we resist it or refuse it? "LORD, you have assigned me my portion and my cup" (Ps. 16:5). When we live by faith, the cup of suffering becomes a "cup of salvation" as we obey him (Ps. 116:13). Yes, there are times when obeying God's will is costly and painful, *but not doing God's will is even more costly and painful.*

When we think about the angels doing the will of God, we must admit and confess our own shortcomings. The angels obey the Lord immediately, without excuse or delay, and they do God's bidding joyfully as they seek to please their Lord. We can't conceive of disagreements or competition among them as they humbly serve together, because their concern is to glorify God. But even more, *their obedience involves the worship and praise of the Lord.* "If God's will is to be done on earth as it is in heaven," wrote P. T. Forsyth, "prayer begins with adoration. . . . We stir up *all that is within us* to bless and hallow God's name."[19] He reminds us that our petitions should be "purified by adoration, praise, and thanksgiving."[20] This may explain why, in the Lord's Prayer, "hallowed be your name" precedes "your will be done." First we worship and then we serve.

Consider these examples from the Scriptures.

Moses had been away from Egypt for forty years. Then he met God at the burning bush, took off his sandals, hid his face, and worshiped. In that awesome meeting, he learned God's name, experienced God's holy power, and surrendered to do God's will and return to Egypt to deliver his people. But the obedience of Moses wasn't a shallow emotional response to the great suffering of Israel in Egypt; it was a heart response to the greatness of God in heaven. Yes, the need was there, but it had to be met by someone whose heart had been moved by worship.

Before he said "Here am I. Send me!" Isaiah saw the Lord "seated on a throne, high and exalted" (Isaiah 6). There wasn't much holiness in the kingdom of Judah, despite their outward show of religion. Isaiah knew that he and his people were sinful, but when he beheld the holiness and greatness of God, his life was transformed. That is what moved him to obey when the Lord asked, "Whom shall I send? And who will go for us?" The need is always great, but it isn't news stories and statistics that should move us to obey God's call. Our motivation must be the greatness and glory of God. "Hallowed be your name . . . your will be done."

When the prophet Habakkuk saw the Babylonian army coming to attack the kingdom of Judah, he questioned the wisdom and justice of God. He talked to the Lord about it (chapter 1) and then quietly listened to God's answer (chapter 2). But the thing that changed the prophet from questioning to rejoicing and from prayer to praise was the revelation of the greatness and glory of God (chapter 3). God revealed his glory to his servant in a storm that left Habakkuk with a pounding heart, quivering lips, and trembling knees (3:16). Habakkuk's confession of faith in 3:16–19 is one of the greatest found in the Scriptures.

Luke records that the Holy Spirit called Paul and Barnabas into wider ministry while the spiritual leaders at the church in Antioch were "worshiping the Lord and fasting" (Acts 13:1–3). While on the Damascus road, Paul had seen Jesus and heard his commission; but it was in a local church worship service that he received the go-ahead signal to begin evangelizing the nations. The result was one of the most remarkable ministries in the history of the Christian church.

What does all of this have to do with knowing and doing the will of God?

I had been ministering many years before I finally had the discernment to understand the important relationship between Romans 11:33–36 and the familiar "dedication invitation" in Romans 12:1–2. I had never connected the two passages! I knew that the chapter break in our translations wasn't put there by Paul, and that the word *therefore* in Romans 12:1 connected the two passages; but I didn't stop to ask why. Here's the way I should have read Romans 11:33–12:2.

> Oh, the depth of the riches of the wisdom and knowledge of God! How unsearchable his judgments, and his paths beyond tracing out! Who has known the mind of the Lord? Or who has been his counselor? Who has ever given to God, that God should repay them? For from him and through him and to him are all things. To him be the glory forever! Amen. Therefore, I urge you, brothers and sisters, in view of God's mercy, to offer your bodies as a living sacrifice, holy and pleasing to God—this is true worship. Do not conform to the pattern of this world, but be transformed by the renewing of your mind. Then you will be able to test and approve what God's will is—his good, pleasing and perfect will.

Before Paul admonishes us to submit ourselves to God as living sacrifices, he first invites us to bring praise to the Lord as adoring worshipers. This benediction contains four verses that we must heed if we are really serious about doing the will of God.

- Don't try to explain God's ways (v. 33). It can't be done. Just do what he says by faith and he will take care of everything. Faith is living without scheming.
- Don't try to change God's mind (v. 34). You'll be the loser.
- Don't try to buy God off (v. 35). His will is nonnegotiable. You don't bargain for God's blessings; you obey his commands.
- Don't try to steal God's glory (v. 36). Then you'll miss everything God wants to give you. He will provide all that you need, but he will never give his glory or praise to anyone else (Isa. 42:8).

Meditate on those four admonitions and you will probably think of people in Scripture or in your circle of family and friends who ignored them and experienced disappointment and difficulty as a result. (Maybe you've done it yourself!) "Before I was afflicted I went astray, but now I obey your word" (Ps. 119:67).

One more consideration: please note that Romans 12:2 says "test and approve what God's will is." The verb *test* means "to discern, to find and to follow," as in testing metals and separating the gold from the dross. It suggests that God's guidance usually involves several factors that must be evaluated carefully, such as circumstances, personal counsel, Scripture, self-examination, and the Spirit's inner direction. The Good Shepherd who died for us also lives for us and wants to guide us, and we can trust him.

The clear statements of God's Word are excellent guides in the everyday decisions of life. For example, nine of the Ten Commandments are repeated in the New Testament epistles for God's people to obey today—the fourth commandment is not—and so we never have to ponder whether it's okay to lie, steal, covet, blaspheme, and so forth. The Beatitudes (Matt. 5:1–12), the works of the flesh and the fruit of the Spirit (Gal. 5:19–26), the evidences of love (1 Corinthians 13), and the practical admonitions of the Word (such as Ephesians 4–6; Phil. 2:1–19; 4:1–9) cover just about every area of the Christian life. God's dealings with Israel in the Old Testament (1 Cor. 10:1–13) and the example and teachings of Jesus in the four Gospels (1 Peter 2:21) certainly reveal what God expects his people to do today.

According to 2 Timothy 3:14–17, the Scriptures are adequate for teaching us, rebuking and correcting us, and training us for our walk, our witness, and our work. In some places the Scriptures boldly say, "This is the will of God." For example, 1 Thessalonians 4:3 says that maintaining personal sexual purity is the will of God. First Timothy 2:4 and 2 Peter 3:9 affirm that it is God's will that sinners trust Christ, so we should not be discouraged in our witnessing. First Peter 2:15 says that doing good works is the way for believers to silence the opposition, and it may even be God's will for us to suffer wrongfully (3:17). Praying for those in authority is the will of God (1 Tim. 2:1–3), although you don't hear that kind of praying very much.

It's also important to be acquainted with the major characters in the Bible, both the wicked and the righteous. By studying their lives, you will discover the basic principles of successful Christian life and service.

One word of caution: some decisions we make are more important than others, so be sensible. I knew a seminary student who prayed about every choice he made—the breakfast cereal he ate, the color of the socks he wore, what corner he should use in crossing the street—and the practice eventually led to a breakdown. Yes, God can and does work in matters that seem unimportant at the time, but this is where we trust him as we walk daily in the Spirit. Years ago I attended a birthday party at which a friend casually suggested I go to seminary with him and be his roommate. It was late in the summer and I didn't think I had any chance of being accepted, *but I was*! It was there I met the girl who has been my wife since 1953. I also made some lifelong friends at seminary, including two professors whose instruction and friendship enriched my ministry immensely.

In 1 Corinthians 10:27, Paul writes, "If an unbeliever invites you to a meal *and you want to go*" (italics added), which suggests that the believer's decision wasn't of an earthshaking nature. How the believer behaves at the meal is Paul's major concern. If we are living in the Word and seeking to glorify Christ, the Spirit will direct us when we must make these "routine" everyday decisions. If we unintentionally begin to move in the wrong direction, the Lord will stop us and instruct us (Phil. 3:12–14). Paul called this "keeping in step with the Spirit" (Gal. 5:25).

When we pray "your will be done on earth," we are praying for ourselves as well as for the church in general. If we permit the peace of God to guard our hearts and minds (Phil. 4:7), the God of peace will guide us. "Show me your ways, LORD, teach me your paths" (Ps. 25:4).

What should we do when we think we're making the right decision only to learn that the Lord has other plans? I once applied for a job and was accepted; but then I had such heaviness in my heart, I knew I'd made a mistake. Immediately I phoned the company and bowed out, and God's peace returned. Shortly after that, a much better situation opened up for me. I was sincere in my praying and planning, but I was also sincerely wrong. "For he knows how we are formed, he remembers that we are dust" (Ps. 103:14).

Take King David, for example, in 2 Samuel 7. He wanted to build a temple for the Lord, and from his many battles he had collected immense wealth to pay for it. He even had the official blessing of Nathan, his court prophet. But the Lord instructed Nathan to tell David he was *not* to build the temple; rather, his son would build it. David's prayer is a perfect example of turning "disappointment into his appointment," as Dr. A. T. Pierson used to express it. *God told David he would build a "house" (family) for him, and from that house the Messiah would be born!* God's denials usually result in special blessings that more than compensate for anything we think we have lost. David submitted to the Lord and made the preparations necessary for Solomon to build God's temple.

Numbers 20 records how Moses lost his temper at Kadesh, struck the rock, and robbed God of the glory only he deserved. Moses also robbed himself of the privilege of leading the nation into the Promised Land. Apparently he prayed more than once that the Lord would allow him to enter Canaan, but this angered God, who told him to stop asking (Deut. 3:23–28). Why was the Lord so hard on Moses? For one thing, if Moses had led Israel into their inheritance, it would have contradicted the teaching in Hebrews 4. That chapter tells us that Joshua is a type of Jesus (his name means "Jehovah is salvation"). Only the grace of Jesus Christ, not the law of Moses, gives us our spiritual inheritance. Jesus is our Joshua who leads us in triumph to claim our rich inheritance (2 Cor. 2:14). But Moses did finally enter the Holy Land! It was on the Mount of Transfiguration where he and Elijah saw the glory of Jesus Christ (Matt. 17:1–13). That experience more than compensated for the blessings he missed at Kadesh.

During his second missionary journey, Paul and his companions wanted to minister in Asia, but God closed the door. He also closed the door when they headed for Bithynia. While waiting at Troas, Paul got his orders from the Lord and went to Philippi, where a new church was established that was close to Paul's heart (Acts 16:6–12). Paul's letter to the Philippians is my favorite epistle, and I would be unhappy if it were not in the New Testament. I'm sure many other people agree with me.

There's a great difference between sincerely making a mistake and deliberately rebelling against God. Moses knew he was commanded to speak to the rock, but he disobeyed and struck the rock, and for this sin he had to be disciplined. When God is not permitted to rule, he often overrules and is able to bring blessing out of disobedience and disappointment.

In this present evil age, we are surrounded by people who ignore or oppose God's will, and even hate God's will, as they try to stop the church from bearing witness to the truth. Their motives are so selfish and their methods so deceptive that it's easy for us to despise them and want to see them removed from the scene. However, the same laws that give Christians the freedom to spread the gospel give these merchandisers of muck the right to peddle their wares. Unfortunately, there are many things that are legal that are not necessarily moral or biblical.

But we must never allow our hearts to become hard and bitter as we witness sinners on earth defying the God of heaven. Jesus wept over the wickedness of Jerusalem in his day (Matt. 23:37–39), and that's a good example for us to follow. So is the example of the writer of Psalm 119:

"Streams of tears flow from my eyes, for your law is not obeyed" (v. 136).

"Rulers persecute me without cause, but my heart trembles at your word" (v. 161).

"Though the arrogant have smeared me with lies, I keep your precepts with all my heart" (v. 69).

"Indignation grips me because of the wicked, who have forsaken your law" (v. 53).

"They almost wiped me from the earth, but I have not forsaken your precepts" (v. 87).

In other words, we should feel anger because of the seeming success of sin while at the same time praying for the sinners. If we react only in anger, we will be fighting the enemy with their own weapons, not the Lord's; but if we respond in agony—which is anger mixed with compassion—we are fighting with God's weapons, as did Jeremiah, "the weeping prophet," centuries ago. (See Jer. 9:1; 10:19; 14:17–18; 23:9–12.)

In spite of the fact that the earth is full of wickedness and violence, as in the days of Noah (Gen. 6:5, 11–12), to those who live by faith "the earth is full of his unfailing love" (Ps. 33:5) and "the whole earth is full of his glory" (Isa. 6:3). We are in partnership with God, praying that his will be done on earth even as it is in heaven. "If God is for us, who can be against us?" (Rom. 8:31).

I'm not personally responsible that the whole earth obey the will of God, but I am responsible to pray this prayer and see to it that *I* obey his will joyfully from my heart (Eph. 6:6). I can either encourage other people or provide them with an excuse, and I want to be an encouragement.

Teach Me Thy Way, O Lord

Teach me Thy Way, O Lord;
Teach me Thy Way!
Thy guiding grace afford,
Teach me Thy Way!
   Help me to walk aright,
   More by faith, less by sight,
   Lead me with heav'nly light;
   Teach me Thy Way!

When I am sad at heart,
Teach me Thy Way!
When earthly joys depart,
Teach me Thy Way!
   In hours of loneliness,
   In times of dire distress,
   In failure or success,
   Teach me Thy Way!

When doubts and fears arise,
Teach me Thy Way!
When storms o'er spread the skies,
Teach me Thy Way!
   Shine through the cloud and rain,
   Thro' sorrow, toil and pain,
   Make Thou my pathway plain;
   Teach me Thy Way!

Long as my life shall last,
Teach me Thy Way!
Where'er my lot be cast,
Teach me Thy Way!
   Until the race is run,
   Until the journey's done,
   Until the Crown is won,
   Teach me Thy Way!

S. Mansell Ramsey

Stewardship

"Give us today our daily bread"

We are now at the heart of the Lord's Prayer. Here we transition from the concerns that relate especially to God's program (Matt. 6:9–10) to the specific needs of God's people (vv. 11–13): sustenance, forgiveness, and protective guidance. *If we are faithful to put God's concerns first, then we are better prepared to speak with him about our own needs.* "But seek first his kingdom and his righteousness, and all these things will be given to you as well" (Matt. 6:33). We should faithfully test our personal prayer requests by God's priorities. If God gave us what we asked, would it glorify his name, advance his kingdom, and accomplish his will on earth? If not, why should we ask?

In the ancient Near East, the word *bread* referred both to food in general and to the flat loaves made from either wheat or barley flour. In that society, bread was the staff of life, and a family was careful to keep fresh bread on hand (see Luke 11:5–13). *Bread* represents all that we need to sustain life as we serve the Lord. Today we can buy bread at a store or go to our freezer and take out a loaf and defrost it, but life wasn't that easy in the ancient world. Each morning family members would put olives, cheese, and perhaps figs into the tortilla-like loaves, fold the bread, and put it into their pockets

91

or bags before heading off to work. The bread was both the lunch and the lunch box. It helped to make it possible for people to earn a living.

Prayer and stewardship go together and must never be separated, for we must make good use of the answers to prayer God graciously gives us. We are stewards of the blessings the Father sends to us day after day. In the ancient world, a steward was a person put in charge of the master's possessions. He or she had the responsibility of guarding those possessions, using them for the profit and pleasure of the master, and keeping accurate accounts for the master to examine. While the steward's position was a privileged one, it came with much responsibility, for the inevitable day of reckoning always came.

The Lord created a marvelous world for our employment and enjoyment (1 Tim. 6:17–19), and we must not carelessly waste God's gracious gifts. God's creation contains everything we need for sustaining life, serving the Lord, and helping others. We are God's stewards, not only of the human, animal, vegetable, and mineral blessings of his "old creation," but also of the spiritual blessings of the "new creation" to which we belong as followers of Jesus Christ (2 Cor. 5:17). One day we will have to give an account of our stewardship before the Lord (Rom. 14:10–12), so we had better be faithful. Let's examine and take to heart the truths involved in this simple but profound request, "Give us today our daily bread."

The word *give* in this request reminds us that we are stewards *by God's grace*. "Every good and perfect gift is from above, coming down from the Father of the heavenly lights, who does not change like shifting shadows" (James 1:17). We see God's grace in *what* God gives us as well as in *the way* God gives it, and we must use these gifts for the good of others and the glory of God. That's what stewardship is all about. The Lord is not obligated to give us anything, yet "in him we live and move and have our being" (Acts 17:28). "You open your hand and satisfy the desires of every living thing" (Ps. 145:16). "And my God will meet all your needs according to the riches of his glory in Christ Jesus" (Phil. 4:19). In ourselves, we are bankrupt, and without God's grace there could be no stewardship. "Everything comes from you, and we have given you only what comes from your hand" (1 Chron. 29:14).

No matter what the situation may be, God is able to care for his children. The Lord is omniscient and knows what we need (Matt. 6:8, 32). He is omnipresent and therefore is with us in every circumstance of life, "an ever-present help in trouble" (Ps. 46:1). He is omnipotent and "able to do immeasurably more than all we ask or imagine" (Eph. 3:20). That word *ask* reminds us that it is through prayer that we tell God what we need. The Father knows our needs better than we do, but he waits for us to ask. True prayer is an act of faith, and God honors faith. "If you believe," said Jesus, "you will receive whatever you ask for in prayer" (Matt. 21:22). Charles Spurgeon was correct when he said, "Whether we like it or not, asking is the rule of the kingdom."[21] James agreed with him: "You do not have because you do not ask God" (James 4:2).

Accustomed as we are to the mouthwatering creations on the bakery or grocery shelf, a piece of bread seems like a lackluster object to us; but actually a piece of bread is a miracle. The poet put it this way:

> Back of the loaf is the snowy flour,
> And back of the flour is the mill;
> And back of the mill is the wheat, sun and shower,
> And the farmer and the Father's will.
>
> Maltbie D. Babcock

Think of it: it requires the cooperation of our universe for us to have a piece of bread. The Lord launched Planet

Earth in just the right orbit around our sun, tilted it carefully, and gave it just the right atmosphere, soils, and amounts of sunlight to sustain human life as we know it. A loaf of bread begins with little seeds of wheat or some other grain that are planted and cultivated and at the right time harvested. The Lord sends the necessary sunshine and rain so that the seeds take root and grow. It requires a combination of the faithfulness and blessing of the Father, as well as the skills and hard work of the farmers, millers, and bakers, to give us a loaf of bread. We hold in our hands a miracle that too often we take for granted.

Many people are blind to this miracle and therefore waste food and throw edible leftovers into the garbage. But in our Lord's time, bread was highly valued and not handled so carelessly. People in the ancient Near East didn't *slice* a loaf of bread; they lovingly *broke* it. To them, slicing a loaf was like stabbing a friend. If they found even a small piece of bread on the ground, they usually picked it up, dusted it off, and put it where a bird or small animal could find it and enjoy it. When Jesus miraculously fed the multitudes, he was careful to have the disciples gather up the leftovers and save them (Matt. 14:20; 15:37), and he expected them to remember how many baskets of leftovers they had collected (Matt. 16:1–12). Jesus wants nothing wasted. Yet in our modern Western world, tons of food are thrown away daily, enough to feed the hungry populations of entire nations.

If we remember that we are stewards because of the grace of God, it will motivate us to cook and eat sensibly and to waste nothing. My preacher uncle, Simon Carlson, followed the Swedish custom of praying *after* meals as well as before, basing it on Deuteronomy 8:10—"When you have eaten and are satisfied, praise the LORD your God." But if we have over-eaten or wasted food, can we really thank the Lord *after* the meal? For what are we grateful and how have we pleased the Lord? Deuteronomy 8:18 says, "But remember the LORD your God, for it is he who gives you the ability to produce wealth."

Wasting food and wasting money are sins in good standing among believers in the Western world and are rarely mentioned at public meetings or in private confession.

Too many people attend church as consumers and not as stewards and worshipers. Church buildings have become shopping malls, not sanctuaries, and "doing church" means "doing business" and not worshiping God or encouraging others. "What's in it for me?" is the most important concern of the average churchgoer, not "How can I become more like Christ and share what I have with others?" If our praying is what it ought to be, we will be transformed from greedy consumers into generous stewards.

It's unfortunate when families argue during meals and fail to act like stewards who are fed by the gracious Lord in heaven. Their table is not an altar of loving worship but a field of intense battle. Better that we don't eat at all than that we eat with a belligerent spirit and fail to eat joyfully and thankfully before the Lord.

The two little words *us* and *our* indicate that we are stewards *along with the people of God*. We have already noted that the Lord's Prayer is a family prayer and we are not solo performers. We may not personally know many of God's people around the world, but we are praying for them and they for us as we pray the Lord's Prayer.

> Before our Father's throne,
> We pour our ardent prayers;
> Our fears, our hopes, our aims are one,
> Our comforts and our cares.
>
> John Fawcett

When Jesus used the phrase "daily bread," the Jewish crowd listening to him surely must have recalled the manna that fell from heaven six days a week as their ancestors wandered in the wilderness (Exodus 16). No matter how much manna each family gathered, nobody had too little or too much (Exod. 16:18), so nothing was wasted. If a family self-ishly tried to store up manna during the week, it bred worms and smelled and had to be thrown away. Only on the sixth day were they allowed to gather extra manna to be set aside to eat on the Sabbath, and that manna didn't spoil. God sent this wonderful "grain of heaven" and "bread of angels" (Ps. 78:24–25) until the Israelites entered the Promised Land, and then the miracle ceased (Josh. 5:10–12). The Hebrew word *manna* simply means "What is it?" The thin, frostlike flakes were a mystery the people couldn't explain, and yet they could eat and be nourished by them day after day.

"So many of us pray because we are driven by need rather than kindled by grace," wrote British theologian P. T. Forsyth,[22] a statement we need to think about often. God is our generous Father, and his Spirit often stirs our hearts just to give thanks to him for his grace. (For an example of a hymn praising the God of all grace, see Ephesians 1:3–14.) Hunger pangs might motivate us to cry out for food or a job, but how much more should we cry out in faith because we depend on God's grace!

In John 6, Jesus preached a sermon in which he compared himself to manna. As a result he lost his congregation (6:66). He called himself "the bread of life" (vv. 35, 48) and "the living bread from heaven" (v. 51), and he told the people they must "believe on him" (vv. 40, 65) and "eat his flesh and drink his blood" (vv. 51–56) if they wanted eternal life. The Jews were commanded never to eat animal blood let alone human blood, and they were so offended at our Lord's words that they rejected him. Of course our Lord was speaking metaphorically: just as Israel ate the manna and it *sustained human life*, so sinners must receive Christ within their hearts and he will *impart eternal life* to them. The manna was sent only to Israel, but Jesus came to offer eternal life to the whole world and to give himself for the world (6:33, 51).[23]

This reminds us that we as God's people must strengthen our spiritual lives by feeding daily on the Word of God. "People do not live on bread alone, but on every word that comes from the mouth of God" (Matt. 4:4; see Deut. 8:3). "I have hidden your word in my heart that I might not sin against you" (Ps. 119:11). Just as the Israelites fed on the manna daily, so we must spend time daily in the Word of God. "When your words came, I ate them; they were my joy and my heart's delight, for I bear your name, LORD God Almighty" (Jer. 15:16). "I have treasured the words of his mouth more than my daily bread" (Job 23:12).

Not only are we stewards *with* God's people, but we are also stewards *of* God's people. That may sound strange, but as members of the family of God and the body of Christ, we belong to each other, we need each other, we influence each other, and in love we should minister to one another. Each of us has different gifts and abilities that we should use for building up one another and the church of Jesus Christ, as evidenced in key passages such as Romans 12, 1 Corinthians 12–14, and Ephesians 4:1–6:9. We should ask God not only to bless others by meeting their needs but also to make us a blessing to others and share what we have. The Lord says to us as he said to Abraham, "I will bless you . . . and you will be a blessing" (Gen. 12:2–3).

This stewardship principle also applies in our relationships to people outside the family of God. Christian teachers in public schools are stewards as they seek to influence and instruct their students, and so are Christian employers who direct the work of their employees (Eph. 6:5–9; Col. 3:18–4:1). As praying believers, do we make it easier for others to do their best and be their best? Do we encourage others or make life more difficult for them? Do we sacrifice for others or happily allow them to sacrifice for us? Do we strive to make others look good? Do we use our authority so that we build others up or only to promote ourselves?

Joseph was a good steward of his opportunities to help the Egyptians and his own brothers. Ten of his brothers had been cruel to him and he had the authority to punish them, but he refused to do so. Instead, he forgave them. He dealt patiently with his brothers until they came to the place of repentance and confession, and then he gave them a new beginning. Joseph knew that it was important to preserve Jacob's family, because God had a great work for the nation of Israel to do in the world. In contrast, David was a poor steward of some of his sons, pampering Absalom, Adonijah, and Amnon and failing to discipline them. Yet David attracted many "mighty men" to his army, men who were willing to lay down their lives for their king (2 Sam. 23:8–39). As devoted friends, David and Jonathan encouraged each other and were willing to sacrifice for each other.

Paul had a host of friends and associates in ministry who loved him, prayed for him, and labored with him in the Lord. He was a blessing to them as they were to him. Yes, he and Barnabas had a falling out over John Mark (Acts 13:13; 15:36–41). But that was eventually settled peacefully (Col. 4:10; 2 Tim. 4:11), and both Mark and Barnabas served God faithfully, as did Paul. The early church worked as a team, and Paul was a wise coach and a great player.

How we relate to others, both saved and unsaved, should be a prayer concern for all of us so we can minister to others. It's much easier for us to ask God to change other people than it is to ask him to change us. What patience Jesus needed as he trained his disciples to continue his work! In three of the Gospels you find him asking, "How long must I put up with you?" (Matt. 17:17; Mark 9:19; Luke 9:41). And think of the grace Jesus demonstrated toward Judas, the deceiver who would betray him. Jesus even washed his feet!

"As iron sharpens iron, so one person sharpens another" (Prov. 27:17). If somebody is being a file or sandpaper in our lives, let's ask God to use the experience to polish us, not to scratch or irritate us.

We exercise our stewardship *a day at a time*, a fact so important it is mentioned twice: "Give us *today* our *daily* bread" (italics added). Greek scholars have wrestled with the word *epiousios*, translated "daily" in the KJV, TNIV, NASB, and NKJV. The word is translated as "for tomorrow," "needful," and "sufficient" in other modern English versions. The word hearkens back to Exodus 16 and the daily manna God gave Israel in the wilderness, as well as to Proverbs 30:8: "Keep falsehood and lies far from me; give me neither poverty nor riches, but give me only my daily bread."

The word *daily* introduces the subject of time, so let's take time to consider time and its relationship to the Christian life. As Henry David Thoreau said in the first chapter of his classic book *Walden*, "As if you could kill time without injuring eternity." Christian believers respect time because the way we use time prepares us for eternity.

Our universe was created a day at a time and it operates a day at a time. No matter how talented or wealthy people may be, nobody can live two days at a time. (There are people who attempt this feat and pay for it with heart attacks or nervous breakdowns or ulcers.) I heard about a cleaning lady who said to one of her customers, "The trouble with life is that it's so daily." *But that's one of the best things about life: it's daily!* If we had to do all our work, carry all our burdens, and make all our decisions at one time, it would crush us. But God has assigned each day its own particular burdens and blessings. One of my favorite Swedish hymns says:

> He whose heart is kind beyond all measure
> Gives unto each day what He deems best—

Lovingly its part of pain and pleasure,
Mingling toil with peace and rest.[24]

Someone has said that the average American is being "crucified" between two thieves: the regrets of yesterday and the worries about tomorrow. While it's foolish to ignore yesterday's costly lessons or tomorrow's important responsibilities, it's also foolish to waste today's opportunities by fretting and worrying instead of acting. In the Sermon on the Mount, Jesus had a great deal to say about worry (Matt. 6:19–34). He pointed out that the Father feeds the birds of the air and clothes the flowers of the field and will do the same for us if we trust him. He made it clear that success in life is a matter of priorities. "But seek first the kingdom of God and his righteousness, and all these things will be given to you as well" (Matt. 6:33). There's that word *give* again. We can't live successfully without God's grace.

"I wish I had more time!" I've said that more than once in my life, and perhaps you have too; but all of us are stewards of twenty-four hours a day. No more, no less. Some years ago I was complaining about my schedule when a friend quietly said, "There's always time for the will of God." Ouch! I complained about my schedule at our family dinner one evening and our younger daughter asked, "Dad, who plans your schedule?" Ouch again!

Back in 1748, Benjamin Franklin published his *Advice to a Young Tradesman* in which he made that famous statement, "Remember that time is money." But time is much more than money. The apostle Paul tells us that time is opportunity!

Be very careful, then, how you live—not as unwise but as wise, making the most of every opportunity, because the days are evil. Therefore do not be foolish, but understand what the Lord's will is.

Ephesians 5:15–16

Note that last phrase: "what the Lord's will is." This takes us back to the third request in the Lord's Prayer: "your will be done, on earth as it is in heaven" (Matt. 6:10). Remember, the will of God is the expression of the love of God for us. Knowing, loving, and doing the will of God is the key to an effective life. When God's priorities are our priorities, we avoid time-wasting detours and make progress on the main road God has assigned us. It isn't usually bad things that take us off the main road, but good things that really aren't on God's agenda for us.

When I read the Gospel records, I'm impressed by the way Jesus did his daily work. He was up early to pray and to receive his Father's orders for the day (Mark 1:35; see Isa. 50:4–5). We don't see any nervous haste or confusion. He always had time for individuals, and occasional interruptions didn't irritate him. (Many of us have learned that the interruptions are usually the ministry!) He was often weary and at least once fell sound asleep during a violent storm while in a boat on the Sea of Galilee. In the midst of the noisy crowds, he was a center of calm; and when he was on trial, his commanding poise amazed both his accusers and his judges. If we would submit ourselves to the control of the Holy Spirit as he did, we could follow his example.

We need to remind ourselves repeatedly that we are God's appointed stewards and that he is prepared to give us what we need so that we may accomplish his will. We are not manufacturers; we are distributors. Our works depend on his grace, and we can't earn grace. "But he gives us more grace" (James 4:6), and we receive it by faith.

Take My Life and Let It Be

Take my life and let it be
Consecrated, Lord, to Thee;
Take my moments and my days—
Let them flow in ceaseless praise,
Let them flow in ceaseless praise.

Take my hands and let them move
At the impulse of Thy love.
Take my feet and let them be
Swift and beautiful for Thee,
Swift and beautiful for Thee.

Take my voice and let me sing
Always, only, for my King.
Take my lips and let them be
Filled with messages from Thee,
Filled with messages from Thee.

Take my silver and my gold—
Not a mite would I withhold.
Take my intellect and use
Ev'ry power as Thou shalt choose,
Ev'ry power as Thou shalt choose.

Take my will and make it Thine—
It shall be no longer mine;
Take my heart—it is Thine own,
It shall be Thy royal throne,
It shall be Thy royal throne.

Take my love—my Lord, I pour
At Thy feet its treasure store;
Take myself—and I will be
Ever, only, all for Thee,
Ever, only, all for Thee.

Frances Ridley Havergal

Fellowship

"Forgive us our debts,
as we also have forgiven our debtors"

How strange that the Lord's Prayer should move from asking for bread to asking for the forgiveness of our sins! But there is in Scripture a remarkable connection between food, sin, and forgiveness; in fact, sinning is sometimes compared to eating. Proverbs 19:28 says that "the mouth of the wicked gulps down evil," and Proverbs 30:20 tells us that the adulterous woman "eats and wipes her mouth and says, 'I've done nothing wrong.'"

Sin came into the human race when our first parents took forbidden food and ate it (Genesis 3). When Joseph dealt with his brothers' sins, he first fed them and then told them he forgave them (Genesis 43–45). Jesus took the same approach with Peter, feeding him breakfast before restoring him to fellowship (John 21). The Lord's Supper focuses on the sacrifice of Jesus, the Lamb of God, who died so that our sins might be forgiven (John 1:29). Simon the Pharisee learned about debts and forgiveness during a Sabbath meal with Jesus (Luke 7:36–50). In the parable of the prodigal son, the forgiving father gave a feast to celebrate the return of his wayward son (Luke 15:11–31). In our Lord's invitation in Revelation 3:20, if we open the door to him, he promises to come into our lives and eat with us. In the ancient Near East, to eat together was a sign of peace and friendship. It was a means of strengthening fellowship.

Asking for daily bread reminds us of God's goodness to us, and Romans 2:4 teaches us that God's kindness is intended to bring sinners to repentance. It worked for the prodigal son. "When he came to his senses, he said, 'How many of my father's hired servants have food to spare, and here I am starving to death!'" (Luke 15:17). It was his father's goodness more than his own badness that motivated the boy to return home, and blessed is that wayward sinner who follows his example! If we have eyes to see, daily bread and God's forgiveness go together.

Food is a tangible thing and a very necessary thing, while forgiveness seems intangible and abstract; but both belong to God's world and both are essential to our well-being. Food is necessary for sustaining human life, and forgiveness is essential for sustaining our relationships with God and with people. Bread feeds us physically, and forgiveness feeds us emotionally and spiritually. Food nourishes us for a time and then we have to eat again. An unforgiving spirit eats away at us like a cancer until we get it out of our system. Resentful people who are angry at others will often either eat too much or not be able to eat at all. When we carry grudges against others, we only hurt ourselves, and to continue in this misery instead of seeking God's forgiveness is folly. Resentment has been described as the act of swallowing poison and hoping it will kill your enemy.

Medical researchers have shown that people who won't forgive others often experience an increased heart rate and high blood pressure, and their bodies become more susceptible to fatigue, colds, and infections. One study indicated that resentful people took 25 percent more medication than people who practiced forgiveness. So, for more reasons than one, we must pray this prayer and follow Paul's counsel in Ephesians 4:32—"Be kind and compassionate to one another, forgiving each other, just as God in Christ forgave you."

The Bible gives us many pictures of sin because the Lord wants us to know that sin is more than a word in a book; it's a horrible force that deceives and destroys. God compares sin to defilement, for David prayed, "Wash away all my iniquity and cleanse me from my sin" (Ps. 51:2). What dirt is to the body, sin is to the soul. Sin is also pictured as darkness. The apostle John warns us that we cannot have fellowship with the Lord or his people if we "walk in darkness" and disobey him (1 John 1:5–7). Sin is a form of bondage: "The evil deeds of the wicked ensnare them; the cords of their sins hold them fast" (Prov. 5:22). Sin is a burden: "My guilt has overwhelmed me like a burden too heavy to bear" (Ps. 38:4). Jesus compared sin to sickness and presented himself as the only physician who could heal sinners (Luke 5:29–31). He also pictured sin as "lostness," for sinners are like lost sheep that can't find their way home (Luke 15:1–7). "We all, like sheep, have gone astray, each of us has turned to our own way; and the LORD has laid on him the iniquity of us all" (Isa. 53:6). "Our own way" is the beginning of trouble.

In the Lord's Prayer, Jesus describes our sins as a debt, and most of his listeners knew that the Aramaic word for sin also meant "debt." In our own day, the word *sin* is barely in the vocabulary, and it is rarely associated with debt. Thomas Jefferson warned America that public debt was "the greatest of the dangers to be feared." An old adage says, "When your outgo exceeds your income, your upkeep is your downfall." For personal debtors, an unmanageable debt could mean the end of their freedom. "They who go a-borrowing, go a-sorrowing," says an old English proverb, and when that was written, there were no credit cards.

A debt is a legal obligation, and every sinner is obligated to the Lord to obey his law and do his will. The English words *owe* and *ought* are cousins. The Old Testament trespass offering (or guilt offering) required the offender not only to bring a proper sacrifice to the Lord but also to make restitution to anybody who had been wronged (see Lev. 5:14–6:17 and 7:1–10). When it comes to our obligations to God, we are so spiritually bankrupt we can't begin to pay for forgiveness or even make adequate restitution for the damage we have done and the pain we have caused. Like the prodigal son, we have to admit our poverty and humbly go to the Father and ask for his forgiveness.

Someone has wisely said, "We may forget our decisions, but our decisions will never forget us." The prophet Nathan told King David a story about a stolen pet ewe lamb, and the king became so angry he cried out, "As surely as the LORD lives, the man who did this must die! He must pay for that lamb four times over, because he did such a thing and had no pity" (2 Sam. 12:5–6). Restoring four beasts for one was demanded by the law (Exod. 22:1). The thief could say "I'm sorry," but that wouldn't make things right with the person he had robbed. Offenders are debtors, bankrupt debtors, and all they can do is throw themselves on the mercy of God.

Sin is a costly debt that keeps accumulating painful interest, *but God forgives the sins of repentant sinners who trust Jesus Christ!* This is the miracle message of the gospel.

"Those who conceal their sins do not prosper, but those who confess and renounce them find mercy" (Prov. 28:13). Our first parents tried to conceal their sin, but the Lord sought them out and dealt with them (Gen. 3:8–13), because when we acknowledge our sins, we have taken the first step toward forgiveness. Adam blamed his wife, Eve blamed the serpent, and the Lord judged all three. The law of Moses hadn't been put in force yet, but the God of truth was still in charge. "For the law was given through Moses; grace and truth came through Jesus Christ" (John 1:17). God must first reveal the truth before he can graciously forgive the sinner. Trying to conceal our sins from the all-knowing Lord seems like an easy way to escape judgment, when in reality it only makes matters worse.

The Bible reveals three aspects of forgiveness, and the first is *the final forgiveness sinners receive when they trust Jesus Christ.* "He forgave us all our sins, having canceled the charge of our legal indebtedness, which stood against us and condemned us; he has taken it away, nailing it to the cross" (Col. 2:13–14). Here is the commercial metaphor again: "canceled the charge of our legal indebtedness." It pictures sin as a debt that somebody has to pay. The good news is that Jesus paid the debt for all our sins when he died on the cross and rose again. "In him we have redemption through his blood, the forgiveness of sins, in accordance with the riches of God's grace" (Eph. 1:7). "Therefore, there is now no condemnation for those who are in Christ Jesus" (Rom. 8:1).

The verb *canceled* literally means "wiped out" and pictures an ancient banker wiping off the amount of the debt written on the sheet of papyrus. Twice David used this image in Psalm 51: "blot out my transgressions" (v. 1) and "blot out all my iniquity" (v. 9). Peter used this concept in one of his early sermons: "Repent, then, and turn to God, so that your sins may be wiped out" (Acts 3:19). David used another picture when he wrote Psalm 103: "As far as the east is from the west, so far has he removed our transgressions from us" (v. 12). The Jews would immediately think of the annual Day of Atonement when the high priest laid his hands on the head of the scapegoat and confessed Israel's sins, and then the goat was taken away into the wilderness, never to be seen again (Lev. 16:20–22). You can measure the distance from the north pole to the south pole but not from east to west. It's a beautiful image of our sins being taken away forever!

The Greek word translated "forgive" also means "to send away." John the Baptist saw Jesus approaching and shouted, "Look, the Lamb of God, who takes away the sin of the world!" (John 1:29). The blood of animal sacrifices only *covered* the sins of the Israelites, but the sacrifice Jesus made on the cross *removes* the sins of the whole world! "And we have seen and testify that the Father has sent his Son to be the Savior of the world" (1 John 4:14). Once we have trusted Jesus as our Savior, we are forgiven and declared righteous in him, and God the Father proclaims, "Their sins and lawless acts I will remember no more" (Heb. 10:17).

But what if we sin after we have been saved?

Final forgiveness is just that—it's final, and it secures our eternal destiny. "I give them eternal life, and they shall never perish; no one will snatch them out of my hand" (John 10:28).

However, every believer knows that the enemies that once enslaved us still tempt us—the world (1 John 2:15–17), the flesh (Gal. 5:16–26), and the devil (1 Peter 5:8–9; and see Eph. 2:1–3). Too often we succumb to temptation and we sin. Our disobedience does not mean we're no longer *accepted* by God; it does mean that we're not *acceptable* to our Father. We haven't lost our membership in the family, but we have damaged our fellowship with the Father and with other children of God.

Picture a family that has just moved into a new house and the landscaping has not yet been completed. There is mud in abundance around the house, and the children are warned to stay out of it. But the temptation is too great, and it isn't long before they and their clothing are stained with mud. They go to the back door and ring the bell and their mother answers. Were the children acceptable? Of course not! Were they accepted and allowed to come in? Absolutely—they belonged to the family! Mother cleaned them up, scolded and perhaps disciplined them, gave them a snack, and put them to bed for their naps. As the children grew older, they worked harder at keeping clean.

Being saved or lost is a matter of life or death (John 5:24; Rom. 6:23). Being an obedient or disobedient child of God is a matter of light or darkness. The apostle John put it this way:

> This is the message we have heard from him and declare to you: God is light; in him there is no darkness at all. If we claim to have fellowship with him and yet walk in the darkness, we lie and do not live out the truth. But if we walk in the light, as he is in the light, we have fellowship with one another, and the blood of Jesus, his Son, purifies us from all sin. If we claim to be without sin, we deceive ourselves and the truth is not in us. If we confess our sins, he is faithful and just and will forgive us our sins and purify us from all unrighteousness. If we claim we have not sinned, we make him out to be a liar and his word is not in us.
>
> 1 John 1:5–10

John is writing about *fellowship* forgiveness. The Greek word *koinonia*—translated as "fellowship"—has made its way into our English vocabulary because of "koinonia groups," believers in local churches who meet to pray and encourage one another. The word means "to have in common." When some believers hear the word *fellowship*, they think only of sitting down for coffee and cake, and certainly God's people may have spiritual fellowship as they enjoy food. But true *koinonia* goes much deeper. Those outside the Christian fellowship are in darkness, but believers are in the light. Believers have been cleansed from sin and walk in truth, while unbelievers are defiled by sin and deceive themselves. Read 2 Corinthians 6:14–7:1 for a vivid description of the contrasts between those within the *koinonia* and those outside. It's important!

Because sin robs us of fellowship with the Lord and his people, you would think this request would be first instead of fifth; for if we have sinned, we are out of fellowship with God and he will not hear and answer. "If I had cherished sin in my heart, the Lord would not have listened" (Ps. 66:18).

More than once as I've been praying privately, the Lord has reminded me of an unconfessed sin, and I've had to deal with it then and there. Answered prayer begins with accepted and acceptable people praying. We feel unworthy to approach the throne, *but we are not unwelcomed*!

This truth is illustrated in the Old Testament tabernacle and temple. The first thing the Israelites saw at the sanctuary was the brazen altar where the sacrifices were slain. At the far end of the sanctuary, inside the tent and in front of the veil, stood the golden altar where the incense was burned twice daily, representing prayer to the Lord. Between these two altars was a large laver (basin) where the priests frequently washed their hands and feet, because they dared not try to serve the Lord while defiled (Exod. 30:1–10, 17–21).

When the mother in my earlier illustration saw her mud-stained children, she accepted them and then made them acceptable. She took off their filthy clothing, bathed them, dressed them with clean clothing, kissed them, probably gave them a snack, and put them to bed. At the brazen altar, the blood of the sacrifice atoned for sin; but at the laver, the defilement of sin was washed away and fellowship was restored. Final forgiveness and fellowship forgiveness go together. When we come to the throne of grace, we may have to interrupt our prayers for others in order to pray for ourselves, and the Father understands.

God's people are not only *forgiven*; they are also *forgiving*. "And forgive us our debts, as we also have forgiven our debtors." Note those plurals, because forgiveness involves the church family; and family forgiveness is as important to building a healthy and happy church as it is to building a healthy and happy home.

The phrase "our debtors" surely reminded Jesus's Jewish listeners of the Year of Jubilee that Israel was supposed to observe every fiftieth year (Lev. 25:8–55). Why? Because during that special year, all debts were forgiven. Any land that had been sold during the previous forty-nine years was to be returned to the original owners, and people who had relocated went back to their original homes. The poor people who had been forced to sell themselves as servants were forgiven their debts and allowed to return home. The words quoted on the Liberty Bell in Philadelphia were heard: "proclaim liberty throughout the land" (Lev. 25:10). The Year of Jubilee marked a new beginning for the people of Israel every fifty years.

The Gospel writers record three instances of how Jesus dealt forcefully with the sin of an unforgiving spirit. In Matthew 18:21–35 Jesus tells about a servant who, even after his master forgave him a huge debt, refused to forgive a fellow servant who owed him a very small amount. Paul may have had this parable in mind when he wrote, "Be kind and compassionate to one another, forgiving each other, just as in Christ God forgave you" (Eph. 4:32).

In Luke 7:36–50, Jesus taught a self-righteous and judgmental Pharisee the meaning of true repentance and forgiveness. While the man saw no sin in himself, he was quick to see a great deal of sin in the woman weeping at the feet of Jesus. When Jesus examined the books, however, Simon was in great debt himself. There are sins of the spirit as well as sins of the flesh (2 Cor. 7:1), and there are sins of omission as well as sins of commission (Luke 7:44–46)—and Simon was guilty!

A third passage is the familiar parable of the prodigal son (Luke 15:11–32). Too often we close our sermons on this text with the homecoming of the younger son, but Jesus went on to talk about the self-righteous older son who would not forgive his brother. As a result, the older son was out of fellowship with his father and his brother and refused to enjoy the feast. The publicans and sinners were represented by the prodigal (Luke 15:1–2) and the self-righteous, unforgiving Pharisees by the older brother, *and both were sinners*! However, the older brother showed no signs of repentance and could not be forgiven. When he closed the door of his heart on his younger brother, he also closed it on his father.

This matter of family forgiveness was so important that Jesus added a postscript to the Lord's Prayer: "For if you forgive others when they sin against you, your heavenly Father will also forgive you. But if you do not forgive others their sins, your Father will not forgive your sins" (Matt. 6:14–15; and see Matt. 18:35 and Mark 11:22–25). It's important to understand that forgiving others isn't a reason for God to forgive us or a device we use to earn his forgiveness. After all, forgiveness is a matter of grace and mercy, not law and good works, and there's no reason for God to forgive us except his great love. If I don't forgive others, I make myself a judge like Simon the Pharisee and the elder brother, instead of being a humble sinner like the prostitute or the prodigal.

King David was a wealthy man and could have sacrificed hundreds of animals to the Lord, but that wasn't what the Lord wanted. "My sacrifice, O God, is a broken spirit; a broken and contrite heart you, God, will not despise" (Ps. 51:17). If my heart is broken over my own sins, it will be broken over the sins of others and I will want the Lord to forgive them as well. Dr. Howard Hendricks said, "Love is the circulatory system of the body of Christ, the church," and Peter wrote, referring to Proverbs 10:12, "Above all, love each other deeply, because love covers over a multitude of sins" (1 Peter 4:8). Love doesn't condone sin but it doesn't advertise it. Love is a wonderful covering.

God forgives us for the sake of his Son, and we must forgive others for the same reason (Eph. 4:32). *If we don't, our unforgiving attitude may lead us into further sin!* "Brothers and sisters, if someone is caught in a sin, you who live by the Spirit should restore that person gently. But watch yourselves, or you also may be tempted" (Gal. 6:1). We must never use the fall of another believer to exalt ourselves and make ourselves look better, saying, "I would never do a thing like that!" Peter spoke like that and went out and sinned. The word *restore* was a medical term that meant "to set a broken bone." Would you want your physician to set your broken leg using a pipe wrench and a sledgehammer? *We must not be gentle with sin, but we must be gentle with sinners.* "So, if you think you are standing firm, be careful that you don't fall!" (1 Cor. 10:12).

Knowing what would happen to Peter on the night of our Lord's arrest, Jesus prayed for him and Peter was eventually restored. Today in heaven, our Lord is interceding for his people, and when we pray for those who have failed, it's good to remember that Jesus prays for them also. The last time we all failed the Lord, he prayed for us and also burdened some of his people to intercede for us in love. If someone has sinned against us, our Lord's counsel in Matthew 18:15–20 gives us the recipe for restoration of fellowship. The Holy Spirit can use our loving humility and honesty to bring about reconciliation and defeat the devil's plans. If family forgiveness were more of a priority in our churches, perhaps there would be fewer church fights and splits.

Forgiveness restores our fellowship with the Lord and with his people. "If we confess our sins, he is faithful and just and will forgive our sins and purify us from all unrighteousness" (1 John 1:9). God is faithful to his people and to his promise to forgive, and he is just toward his Son who died for our sins. "Blessed are those whose transgressions are forgiven, whose sins are covered. Blessed are those whose sin the LORD does not count against them and in whose spirit is no deceit" (Ps. 32:1–2).

At first David tried to cover up his adultery by being deceitful, and when that didn't work, he had Bathsheba's husband Uriah killed on the battlefield (2 Sam. 11:6–27). The last sentence in that chapter is ominous: "But the thing David had done displeased the LORD." We cannot please ourselves with sin and please God at the same time, because "our fellowship is with the Father and with his Son, Jesus Christ" (1 John 1:3). Our fellowship is also with the Holy Spirit, who dwells within us (2 Cor. 13:14; Phil. 2:1). God is light, and we cannot walk with him if we're in the darkness of disobedience.

One of the tragic consequences of broken fellowship is our inability to pray and receive answers. "If I regard wickedness in my heart, the Lord will not hear" (Ps. 66:18 NASB). The word translated "regard" means "to know it is there and approve of it." Unconfessed sin is a barrier to answered prayer. "For the eyes of the Lord are on the righteous and his ears are attentive to their prayer, but the face of the Lord is against those who do evil" (1 Peter 3:12). Marital disagreements can hinder husbands and wives from seeing their prayers answered (1 Peter 3:7), and neglecting God's Word will also hinder a person's prayer life (Prov. 28:9). "If you abide in Me, and My words abide in you, ask whatever you wish, and it will be done for you" (John 15:7 NASB).

But there are also tragic consequences to *forgiven sin*. When God forgives us, he pulls the nails out of the board *but he does not remove the holes*. God's children must reap what they sow. When David told Nathan, "He must pay for that lamb four times over" (2 Sam. 12:5–6), he actually passed judgment on himself. Four of his sons died: Bathsheba's baby, Amnon, Absalom, and Adonijah. Stealing Uriah's "little ewe lamb" was a costly experience for David.

However, God didn't abandon David. He stayed with him during all the trials his sons brought to the family, and he never revoked his covenant with David or any of the promises he had made. God had allowed David to amass great wealth to be used in building the temple. He also gave David the blueprints for the temple (1 Chron. 28:11–19) and another son—Solomon—who completed the work. When we don't permit God to rule, he will overrule us and accomplish his great purposes anyway, but there will be a greater price for us to pay.

Losing the blessings of fellowship with God and his people is not worth enjoying "the fleeting pleasures of sin" (Heb.

11:25). Knowing that the Spirit of God is working in us and through us, that we are peacemakers and not troublemakers, that God is speaking to us from his Word, and that we are helping to advance the work of God and magnify the glory of God are reasons for great joy, no matter what our circumstances might be. Believers who refuse to confess their sins or to forgive the sins of others only rob themselves of the blessings God has prepared for them.

There is a beautiful promise in Joel 2:25 that helps to heal the wounds of believers who have disobeyed the Lord, suffered for it, and then confessed their sins and been restored: "I will repay you for the years the locusts have eaten." In Joel's day, the land had suffered a devastating invasion of locusts, God's judgment on his sinning people. Through the prophet the Lord pleaded with the people to repent and return to him, promising that he would forgive them and even compensate for all that they had lost. God can cleanse and God can restore.

On Sunday evening, May 30, 1886, Charles Spurgeon preached from that text and said to his congregation in the Metropolitan Tabernacle in London:

> Lost years can never be restored literally. Time once past is gone forever. . . . You cannot have back your time; but there is a strange and wonderful way in which God can give back to you the wasted blessings, the unripened fruits of years over which you mourned. The fruits of wasted years may yet be yours. . . . "All things are possible to him that believeth."[25]

Do we deserve this kind of blessing? Of course not! It's pure grace from start to finish. Our God is "the God of all grace" (1 Peter 5:10) and "he gives us more grace" (James 4:6).

Depth of Mercy

Depth of mercy! Can there be
Mercy still reserved for me?
Can my God His wrath forbear—
Me the chief of sinners spare?

I have long withstood His grace,
Long provoked Him to His face,
Would not hearken to His calls,
Grieved Him by a thousand falls.

Now incline me to repent;
Let me now my sins lament;
Now my foul revolt deplore,
Weep, believe and sin no more.

There for me the Savior stands,
Holding forth His wounded hands;
God is love! I know, I feel!
Jesus weeps and loves me still.

Charles Wesley

Discipleship I

"Lead us not into temptation"

We have reached the last of the three requests that relate to our needs as believers.

The request for bread deals with our present needs and the request for forgiveness with our past sins. Now we have before us the request for guidance and protection, which involves our future activities. When we pray "lead us," we are submitting ourselves to Jesus Christ as his disciples, for a disciple is a follower. " 'Come, follow me,' Jesus said [to Peter and Andrew], 'and I will send you out to fish for people.' At once they left their nets and followed him" (Matt. 4:19–20).

At once they became disciples! The crisis of the call led to the process of learning and living that is discipleship. Peter and Andrew didn't ask how many hours they would serve each day or what the fringe benefits were, nor did they ask for a contract. They simply obeyed. Until that day, they had been their own bosses, but now Jesus would be giving the orders. "The first duty of every soul," wrote P. T. Forsyth, "is not to find its freedom but its Master."[26] When Jesus is our Master, we have in him the freedom we need to live, serve, and grow. We are free to experience all that will make us what we were born to become. "You are Simon son of John. You will be called Cephas—a rock" (John 1:42).

The prayer begins with "Our Father" and climaxes with Jesus, our Master. Our relationship is one of love, so there's nothing to fear. "My son, give me your heart and let your eyes delight in my ways" (Prov. 23:26). True discipleship involves giving all that we are and have for all of our life so we can receive all that God has planned for us. Perhaps the best modern equivalent of *disciple* would be *apprentice*, for apprentices love their work and their mentor, and they learn by listening, watching, and obeying. Jesus taught his disciples God's truth, they watched him as he ministered to various kinds of people in different circumstances, and then he sent them out to serve and find out for themselves how much they had really learned. The historian Will Durant was correct when he wrote, "Education is a progressive discovery of our own ignorance." The disciples' ignorance was exposed for all to see whenever one of them tried to tell Jesus what to do.

The word translated "temptation" in Matthew 6:13 can also mean "trial" or "testing." James 1:13 makes it clear that "God cannot be tempted by evil, nor does he tempt anyone." James opened his letter by exhorting his readers, "Consider it pure joy, my brothers and sisters, whenever you face trials of many kinds, because you know that the testing of your faith produces perseverance. Let perseverance finish its work so that you may be mature and complete, not lacking anything. . . . Blessed are those who persevere under trial, because when they have stood the test, they will receive the crown of life that God has promised to those who love him" (1:2–4, 12).

The Father never tempts his children to do evil. However, he does test our faith, because a faith that can't be tested can't be trusted. Faith is only as good as the object of that faith, and our faith is in the one true and living God, the Father and the Son and the Holy Spirit. Whenever anyone makes a profession of faith in Jesus Christ, they will soon enter a time of trial and testing so they can learn whether or not their faith is real. In the parable of the sower (Matt. 13:1–9, 18–23), Jesus pointed out that there are people who "hear the word and at once receive it with joy." But the soil of their hearts is shallow and their faith has no roots; therefore, their response is emotional and temporary. "But when the sun came up, the plants were scorched, and they withered because they had no root" (Matt. 13:6). *Sunshine is good for plant life only if the plants have roots. Trials bring blessings to true Christians but not to shallow "professors."*

God's true children benefit from trials. They have their roots in God's Word, and trials only deepen those roots. Paul and Barnabas said, "We must go through many hardships to enter the kingdom of God" (Acts 14:22). "In this world you will have trouble," Jesus told his disciples. "But take heart! I have overcome the world" (John 16:33). In my years of ministry, I have known people who were zealous for the Lord for a short time and then cooled off and went their own way. They didn't lose their salvation. They never had it.

"[E]ach of you is tempted," James wrote, "when you are dragged away by your own evil desire and enticed. Then, after desire has conceived, it gives birth to sin; and sin, when it is full-grown, gives birth to death" (1:14–15). *How we respond to trials will determine whether or not they test us or tempt us, build us up or tear us down.* The wrong kind of responses will transform trials into temptations. Then our own desires will entice us, and we will abandon prayer and God's promises and disobey the Lord. In that way lies grief, not growth.

The Bible gives us many examples of true believers who didn't persevere under testing and instead "gave birth" to sin because they failed to trust God.

Let's begin with Abraham (Genesis 12). "The God of glory appeared to our father Abraham," Stephen reminded the Jewish Sanhedrin (Acts 7:2), and when that happened, Abraham abandoned his idols, trusted the true God, and started off for the land God promised him. When he arrived there, he discovered a famine in the land. Surely the Lord wouldn't send his child into a famine! Instead of building an altar and waiting for God's directions, Abraham escaped to the land of Egypt, where he almost lost his wife. Instead of trusting God, he lied about his wife and lost his testimony before a pagan ruler and his court. This is a lesson all believers must learn: *faith is living without scheming.* Abraham sinned because he turned a trial into a temptation.

The people of Israel refused to enter the Promised Land (Numbers 13–14), so God chastened them by making them wander in the wilderness for thirty-eight years until the older generation died off. During that "extended funeral march," God often tested his people, and very often they failed the test. As circumstances became difficult, the people usually complained to God and criticized Moses instead of turning to God by faith and praising him. They stood frightened at the Red Sea because Pharaoh's army was coming up behind them; and then God opened the sea and they passed through (Exodus 14–15). When they were hungry, they wept and said, "If only we had died at the Lord's hand in Egypt!" For the next thirty-eight years, God sent them manna to eat (Exodus 16). When they were thirsty, they argued with Moses, who cried out to God and then brought water out of the rock (Exod. 17:1–7). The people as a whole resisted the authority God had given to Moses, and once even his own brother and sister opposed him.

Why did the Lord permit these times of difficulty? Moses tells us in Deuteronomy 8: God was testing the Israelites and revealing their own sinfulness to them. He was encouraging them to trust him and not be afraid. These times of testing could have been a means of grace and blessing that would have increased their faith and their love for God. But their hearts were full of unbelief and their constant prayer was "*How* can we get out of this?" instead of "*What* can we get out of this?" They wanted to go back to Egypt and settle for slavery instead of following God's leading, growing in grace, and inheriting their land.

Moving to the New Testament, we see the disciples in a boat on the Sea of Galilee during a storm, but Jesus is not with them (Matt. 14:22–33). At dawn Jesus shows up, walking on the water, and the disciples are terrified. They had already seen him calm a storm (Matt. 8:23–27), and he had just fed five thousand people with five loaves and two fish, but the disciples' faith was still small. Peter had faith enough to get out of the boat and walk on the water to Jesus, but then he was distracted by the dangerous circumstances around him, turned a test into a temptation, and began to sink.

Let's move to Acts 12 and look at a contrasting experience in Peter's life. He has been arrested and put into jail and is guarded by sixteen Roman soldiers. The next morning he is to be killed. What does Peter do? *He goes to sleep!* He was in such a deep sleep that the angel had to strike Peter on the side to wake him up! (Imagine having an angel for an alarm clock!) Why was Peter so calm? Because he knew Herod could never kill him. Jesus had already told Peter he would die by crucifixion in his old age (John 21:18–19). Peter's faith was tested, and this time he passed the test. He didn't doubt God's promises and turn the trial into a temptation.

Acts 16 gives us another prison testing, this time involving Paul and Silas. Paul was a Roman citizen and could have escaped the pain and humiliation of a beating and a night in prison. Instead, he chose to suffer for the sake of the infant church he and Silas had planted in Philippi. Rather than complaining, the two men prayed and sang praises to the Lord, and the Lord set them free. They turned the testing into triumph and not only were delivered from prison but had the joy of leading the jailer and his household to faith in Jesus Christ.

The key, of course, is faith. If as Jesus's disciples we follow him and do his will, *he promises to take care of us.* If we respond by complaining and scheming ("How can I get out of this?"), we turn the trial into a temptation and our unbelief limits what the Lord can do. How many times has the Lord said to us, "You of little faith, why are you so afraid?" (Matt. 8:26). Faith means obeying God's will no matter how we feel, no matter what the circumstances are around us, and no matter what consequences lie before us. To walk by sight instead of by faith (2 Cor. 5:7) means looking within, looking around, and looking ahead—and being afraid! Throughout Scripture this one fact stands out: *Every believer who was used of God was tested, and they trusted God and did not turn their trials to temptations. To the glory of God, they did the impossible!*

So when we pray "lead us not into temptation," we're saying to the Lord, "Give me the faith I need to accept this trial and use it for your glory. Deepen my roots, increase my faith, and help me turn this testing into triumph and not temptation." Then we rest on his Word, because that is the source and strength of our faith.

It isn't a sin to be tempted or to be tested, but it is a sin to complain and scheme instead of asking the Father for faith to overcome (1 Cor. 10:13). "Lead us not into temptation" means "As we, your disciples, follow you, may we respond in such a way that we not turn opportunities of testing and growth into tragedies of temptation and defeat." The godly Scottish pastor Samuel Rutherford once wrote to a friend, "It is faith's work to claim and challenge lovingkindnesses out of all the roughest strokes of God." After all, that's what Jesus did throughout his ministry, and especially on the cross.

Peter gives us a word of encouragement in 1 Peter 1:6—"In this you greatly rejoice, even though now for a little while, if necessary, you have been distressed by various trials" (NASB). To begin with, the Lord never permits temptations or trials unless they are necessary. We may not understand why God allows us to suffer, but we don't live on explanations—we live on promises. Early in the Lord's Prayer we pray "Your will be done," and if we really mean that prayer, we will accept what he sends us and by faith transform trials into triumphs, not temptations.

Second, God knows how much we can take and therefore how long our trials should last. Paul makes that clear in 1 Corinthians 10:13: "No temptation [testing] has overtaken you except what is common to us all. And God is faithful; he will not let you be tempted [tested] beyond what you can bear. But when you are tempted [tested], he will also provide a way out so that you can endure it."

Third, our trials may distress us, but there is always cause for rejoicing. While we are human and we feel pain, God can enable us to rise above pain and perplexity and to rejoice in him and all that we have in Christ. To quote P. T. Forsyth again, "It is a greater thing to pray for pain's conversion than for pain's removal."[27] Paul pleaded three times that God would remove his painful thorn in the flesh, but instead God converted the pain into power and transformed Paul's weakness into strength (2 Cor. 12:1–10). What a conversion experience that is!

For us to abandon faith and turn life's trials into temptations means not only that we tempt ourselves but also that we tempt the Lord's people *and perhaps even the Lord.* Defeated Christians waste their opportunities for growing in grace, glorifying God, and bearing witness to Jesus Christ and the gospel. Instead of being stepping-stones and bringing people closer to Jesus, they become stumbling blocks that cause others to fall. According to Luke 17:1–3, it's a serious matter to cause other people to stumble.

To tempt God means to behave in such a self-centered and arrogant way that we are daring the Lord to stop us. It means deliberately disobeying him so that he must intervene in some way to keep us from harming ourselves and others and getting in the way of what he wants to do. When Abraham went to

Egypt, God had to intervene to protect him and Sarah so that they could one day bring Isaac into the world. The day after God judged Israel because they refused to enter Canaan, the people decided to "go it alone," and they were humiliated and beaten by the enemy (Num. 14:39–45). Their "attack" was presumptuous sin, not an act of faith in the will of God.

New Testament Christians can tempt God and grieve him just as the Old Testament Israelites did. "Today, if you hear his voice, do not harden your hearts as you did in the rebellion, during the time of testing in the wilderness, where your ancestors tested and tried me, though for forty years they saw what I did. That is why I was angry with that generation" (Heb. 3:7–10; see also Ps. 95:8–10 and 1 Cor. 10:6–10). Imagine God being angry with an entire generation! God called Israel's years in the wilderness "the time of testing" and "the rebellion." What should have been a victory march became a funeral march.

It's serious to play with sin and tempt ourselves (Prov. 7:6–27), and it's dangerous to tempt other people; but it's disastrous to defy God and tempt him. The most severe judgment God can permit is to let us have our own way.

How will Jesus characterize our lives when he reviews them at his judgment seat? Will he see them as years of testing and rebellion, or years when he smiled upon us and was pleased with us?

The Father wants to lead us, but how does he do it? Primarily he leads us from the inspired Word of God as we are taught by the Holy Spirit in fellowship with his people. Remember that the key pronoun in this prayer is *us* and not *me*. Throughout the centuries the Spirit has given teachers to the church, and the written records of their experiences and their expositions of Scripture are a treasury of truth for those who will mine them. This doesn't mean that what they wrote is equal to the Scriptures in accuracy and authority, but only that we can learn from others as we follow the Lord. We need each other as we walk life's path.

King David understood this when he wrote Psalm 23:3— "He guides me along the right paths for his name's sake." The Hebrew word translated "paths" means "deep ruts such as caused by a heavily-loaded cart." The way of safety and blessing is a well-traveled way in the deep ruts that have been proved by God's people for centuries. *Beware of new and easy paths that contradict the old paths trodden by the heroes of the Bible and church history!* "My steps have held to your paths," wrote David; "my feet have not stumbled" (Ps. 17:5). There are modern paved paths that are shallow and devious, and we must avoid them (see Proverbs 2, especially v. 15). "Give careful thought to the paths for your feet," warns Proverbs 4:26, not only because God is watching us (Prov. 15:3) but also because others are following us, and we don't want to lead them astray. The broad road that leads to destruction is popular and pleasant, but the narrow road that leads to life is a deep rut that is unpopular and difficult (Matt. 7:13–14). But it is the safest and happiest place to be for Christians who want to honor the Lord.

I'm grateful to the Lord for Christians who introduced me to some of the "deep ruts" early in my Christian life. This includes the couple who gave me a volume of Spurgeon's sermons when I was in high school, a friend who told me about Bonar's *Memoir and Remains of Robert Murray M'Cheyne*, my Uncle Simon who gave me a copy of Campbell Morgan's *The Crises of the Christ*, and my girlfriend (later my wife) who honored my twenty-first birthday with a copy of *Hudson Taylor's Spiritual Secret*. Over these many years of preaching, teaching, and writing, I have devoted myself to challenging Christians in general and younger pastors in particular to get off the easy detours and move into the deeper ruts on the path of God's choosing.

Please notice *why* we obey God and walk in the deep ruts and not on the enticing new detours: it is "for his name's sake"

(Ps. 23:3). God is glorified when we immerse ourselves in his Word, love it, learn from it, and obey it. He is glorified when we become acquainted with the spiritual leaders he blessed and used in the past, people who have walked in these ruts and have so much to teach us—Augustine, Wesley, Spurgeon, Jonathan Edwards, Amy Carmichael, Frances Ridley Havergal, Oswald Chambers, to name but a few.[28]

Read what Charles Haddon Spurgeon had to say about walking in the "deep ruts" with the giants of the past:

> It seems odd, that certain men who talk so much of what the Holy Spirit reveals to themselves, should think so little of what he has revealed to others. . . . The temptations of our times lie rather in empty pretentions to novelty, than in a slavish following of accepted guides. A respectable acquaintance with the opinions of the giants of the past, might have saved many an erratic thinker from wild interpretations and outrageous inferences.[29]

We will not turn trials and testings into temptations if we stay in the right ruts, and the Holy Spirit of God is with us to help us.

O Breath of Life

O Breath of life, come sweeping through us,
Revive Thy church with life and power.
O Breath of life, come, cleanse, renew us,
And fit Thy church to meet this hour.

O Wind of God, come bend us, break us,
Till humbly we confess our need;
Then in Thy tenderness remake us,
Revive, restore, for this we plead.

O Breath of Love, come breathe within us,
Renewing thought and will and heart;
Come, Love of Christ, afresh to win us,
Revive Thy church in every part.

O Heart of Christ, once broken for us,
'Tis there we find our strength and rest;
Our broken contrite hearts now solace,
And let Thy waiting church be blest.

Revive us, Lord! Is zeal abating
While harvest fields are vast and white?
Revive us, Lord, the world is waiting,
Equip Thy church to spread the light.

Bessie P. Head

Discipleship II

"Deliver us from the evil one"

Satan has been caricatured so much over the centuries that most people don't take him seriously or even believe he exists. To them Satan is a myth, an ugly red creature with a forked tail, pointed ears, and a malicious smile who carries a pitchfork. The Bible paints an entirely different picture, and it's nothing to laugh at.

One of Satan's titles is "the tempter" (Matt. 4:3; 1 Thess. 3:5). Whether he comes as a serpent to deceive (2 Cor. 11:3) or a lion to devour (1 Peter 5:8), Satan roams throughout the earth opposing God's work and tempting God's people to disobey. "Put on the full armor of God, so that you can take your stand against the devil's schemes. For our struggle is not against flesh and blood, but against the rulers, against the authorities, against the powers of this dark world and against the spiritual forces of evil in the heavenly realms" (Eph. 6:11–12).[30] If we want to remain standing in this battle and be able to withstand the enemy, we must by faith put on all the defensive armor God provides and take the weapons of the Word of God and prayer to use offensively against Satan (Eph. 6:13–20; see Acts 6:4). God equips and enables us if we trust him.

I doubt whether Satan has ever personally opposed me and my ministry, or that his demonic forces even know my name. Unfortunately I'm not that big a threat to their operation. "Jesus I know, and I know about Paul, but who are you?" (Acts 19:15). Satan is a created being, which means he isn't omnipresent, as is the Lord God Almighty. If Satan is at work in Chicago, he can't be causing trouble in London or Berlin, except through his agents. The devil appears to be omnipresent because his demonic assistants are constantly busy all over the world. The tempter has probably assigned one of his apprentice demons to tempt me and interfere with my life and work, but I still have to watch and pray if I expect to "stand" and "withstand" as I fight the battle together with the saints (Eph. 6:13).

As Christian believers, we have every right to pray against the devil and ask God to "deliver us from the evil one." Satan and his army are too strong for us but not for God. Jesus commands us to pray for deliverance, and he himself prayed for us that we would have victory. "My prayer is not that you take them [believers] out of the world but that you protect them from the evil one" (John 17:15). Jesus intercedes for us today, and if we trust him and join our prayers with his, he will give us the victory. The Lord "has rescued us from the dominion of darkness and brought us into the kingdom of the Son he loves" (Col. 1:13). We don't fight *for* victory but *from* victory, the victory Christ won for us on the cross. "And having disarmed the powers and authorities, he made a public spectacle of them, triumphing over them by the cross" (Col. 2:15).

The enemy is already at work in and through the lives of lost sinners and disobedient believers. If we are obedient disciples, then the devil will attack us and try to move us out of God's will. He certainly attacks our prayer life and Bible study because he knows that the Word of God and prayer are the most powerful weapons we possess for opposing him and his army. In recent years, churches by the hundreds have eliminated regular prayer meetings, and Satan must be happy about that.

Basically Satan is a counterfeiter and has no original ideas. He takes what the Lord says and offers us substitutes for the true blessings God wants to give us. Read Genesis 3:1–7 and notice how Satan deceived Eve and then used her to tempt Adam. "If the Father loves you so much, why has he forbidden you to eat of the tree? Did God really say that? The Lord is holding out on you!" When Jesus was tempted in the wilderness, the enemy used a similar approach (Matt. 4:1–4). "Your Father just said that you are his beloved Son. Then why are you hungry? If he loved you, surely he would feed you. Turn these stones into bread. Use your power for yourself, not for others."

When we pray "Our Father," we must believe what we are saying, that our Father does love us and will provide for us. The word *our* reminds us that his people are also there to help us in our needs. Otherwise one of Satan's demonic servants will be on hand to tell us that his master cares for us more than God does and that the believers in our lives don't care at all. The father of lies (John 8:42–47) wants to replace the heavenly Father, the God of truth; and Satan's counterfeit Christians want to be on hand to replace the fellowship of true believers (Matt. 13:7, 36–39). Satan promises to give us just what we need, but in the end he takes away far more than he gives. Jesus saves the best wine until the last (John 2:1–10); Satan starts with the best he has but ends with poison.

We must never forget those two little words *our* and *us*. They remind us that we are not fighting alone (1 Peter 5:8–9). Satan hates the church and uses every weapon available to deceive it, defile it, divide it, disgrace it, and destroy it. He especially enjoys using believers in the church to do his dirty work, as he did with Ananias and Sapphira (Acts 5) and the troublemakers in the church in Corinth (1 Cor. 1:4–17;

5:1–6:20). If he can infiltrate the church with his agents, he can work from the inside and do terrible damage (Phil. 3:17–21; 2 Tim. 3:1–9; 2 Peter 2:1–22).

✦✦✦✦✦

Have you ever considered the Lord's Prayer from Satan's point of view? To him the words "Our Father in heaven" are a declaration of war, not a declaration of faith. God is our Father, "the Father of compassion and the God of all comfort" (2 Cor. 1:3), while Satan is a murderer and "the father of lies" (John 8:44). We are part of the church that Jesus is building and that Satan cannot overcome (Matt. 16:18). The Father and the Son are enthroned in heaven and giving us all we need to keep on building and battling until Jesus comes.

When we pray "hallowed be your name," it must infuriate Satan and his demonic army, because Satan's consuming passion is to make himself "like the Most High" (Isa. 14:14). According to Matthew 4:8–10, *Satan wants us to worship him!* According to Revelation 9:20 and chapters 13–14, the unsaved world will one day believe Satan's lies and worship him, and this will ultimately bring them to hell. Why would the world follow Satan? Because unsaved people put security and material possessions ahead of the kingdom of God. They take the easy way, which ultimately becomes the hard way that leads to destruction.

The church has been praying "your kingdom come" for centuries, and though Satan convinces some people that Jesus will not come (2 Peter 3), *the Lord will keep his promises and return!* The day will come when loud voices in heaven will announce, "The kingdom of the world has become the kingdom of our Lord and of his Messiah, and he will reign for ever and ever" (Rev. 11:15). This request focuses our hearts on our future hope, and this is a posture Satan despises. *Hope is confidence ignited by joy.* "But the day of the Lord will come like a thief" (2 Peter 3:10). Christians who live in the future tense experience the joy of the Lord and find strength (Neh. 8:10).

"Your will be done" is a key request that the enemy hates. Jesus made this his prayer in the garden as he faced the cross, and he admonished Peter, James, and John, "Watch and pray so that you will not fall into temptation" (Matt. 26:41). Instead, they went to sleep. When the mob came to arrest Jesus, Peter tried to defend him, and then all the disciples fled. Jesus warned his disciples to go away immediately (John 18:8), but Peter and John followed the mob to the high priest's house, and there Peter denied the Lord three times. Had they joined Jesus in praying "your will be done," they would have obeyed him and not failed in their assignment.

God's will is discovered in God's Word, and Satan wants to keep us from God's Word. If we read the Scriptures daily and meditate on them, then Satan tries to keep the seed of the Word from bearing fruit (Matt. 13:18–23). God reveals his will to those who pray, and sometimes we must "wrestle [agonize] in prayer" as we seek his will (Col. 4:12). If we want deliverance from Satan and his agents, we must feed on the Word, fellowship with God's people, pray earnestly, and seek to glorify God. If we do, Satan will mark us as tough targets and assault us even more, but the Lord will give us victory.

That covers the first three requests in the Lord's Prayer, requests that focus primarily on God and his desires. But Satan attacks our personal prayer requests as well.

When we pray "Give us today our daily bread," the Lord promises to meet our needs. He will provide our daily food, even if he has to enlist birds to help him, as he did for Elijah (1 Kings 17). Jesus began his ministry by fasting, and Satan used that situation to tempt him. If Jesus had taken the approach of some believers, he could have said, "I need bread, I desire it, and I deserve it, so there's nothing wrong in doing it." Satan often appeals to the natural human appetites God has given us, and we must be careful how we respond.

Satan doesn't want us to experience the forgiveness of sins. God says of his children, "Their sins and lawless acts I will remember no more" (Heb. 10:17), but Satan is the accuser of God's people (Rev. 12:10) and attempts to remind us of our mistakes and sins. This may be what Paul means by "the flaming arrows of the evil one" in Ephesians 6:16. I have felt the devil's accusations even while standing in the pulpit preaching God's Word! During those times we must take up the shield of faith and trust God's promises that our sins are held against us no more and that we cannot be condemned (Rom. 8:1). "I, even I, am he who blots out your transgressions, for my own sake, and remembers your sins no more" (Isa. 43:25). When you recall a sin you've committed but have confessed (1 John 1:9), don't dwell on it. Instead, thank God for his forgiveness and praise him for being such a merciful God. For "as far as the east is from the west, so far has he removed our transgressions from us" (Ps. 103:12). Psalm 32 and 1 John 1 are good reminders that God does not hold our confessed sins against us.

The enemy wants to argue with us about how we have treated those who have sinned against us. Jesus commands us to forgive them, but Satan will oppose this response. "After what she did to you, she doesn't deserve forgiveness." Does anybody deserve forgiveness? Of course not! This is where God's mercy and grace come in. Cultivating an unforgiving spirit only fertilizes the soil of the heart so it can produce bitter roots that will poison our lives and defile others (Heb. 12:14–15). But let's remember Jesus's prayer on the cross when he said, "Father, forgive them, because they do not know what they are doing" (Luke 23:34). Or Stephen's prayer as the angry mob stoned him, "Lord, do not hold this sin against them" (Acts 7:60).

The enemy doesn't want us to pray for God's leading or for deliverance from his snares. He prefers that we feel confident and capable of handling whatever comes our way. Peter said to Jesus, "I will lay down my life for you" (John 13:37) and tried to prove it with his sword, but a few hours later he had denied the Lord three times and sat alone weeping. "So, if you think you are standing firm, be careful that you don't fall" (1 Cor. 10:12). Our Lord's frequent admonition to watch and pray reminds us that Satan's devices are subtle and we can't successfully follow the Lord with our eyes closed.

Let's keep "fixing our eyes on Jesus" (Heb. 12:2), not on Satan or on ourselves and our circumstances. The enemy may come as an angel of light and deceive us (2 Cor. 11:13–15). For every lie that Satan tells, we have Bible truth with which to answer him. For every "bargain" he offers us, we have a precious blessing from the Lord that is far better. We must not turn trials into temptations by questioning the love of the Father or trying to scheme our way out of difficult circumstances. Above all, let's remain humble before the Lord and trust him to do what is best for us. "The tail feathers of pride should be pulled out of our prayers," wrote Charles Haddon Spurgeon, "for our prayers need only the wing feathers of faith."[31] John agrees with him: "This is the victory that has overcome the world, even our faith" (1 John 5:4).

Most of us know what sin or sins will tempt us, so we must be careful not to get careless and tempt ourselves. Sometimes the enemy surprises us, but it's more likely he will use the same bait that has already proved successful. For example, Samson knew that as a Nazirite he wasn't supposed to touch a dead body, but he scooped honey out of a lion carcass anyway (Judges 14). After all, he was hungry, and a man has to live. But that act was the beginning of the lying and lusting that ultimately led to Samson's defeat and death.

Lot knew that the cities of the plain were saturated with sin, but he moved into Sodom and eventually sat in the gate of Sodom as one of the city officials. He should have remained with his uncle Abraham, but he had different plans. God's judgment fell on the cities and Lot lost everything (Gen.

13:1–13; 19:1–38). Had it not been for Abraham's intercession with the Lord, Lot would have died in that fiery holocaust.

As we seek God's guidance and his protection from sin and the evil one, let's remember these words of wisdom: "The prudent see danger and take refuge, but the simple keep going and pay the penalty. Humility is the fear of the LORD; its wages are riches and honor and life" (Prov. 22:3–4).

Am I a Soldier of the Cross?

Am I a soldier of the cross—
    A follower of the Lamb?
And shall I fear to own His cause
    Or blush to speak His name?

Must I be carried to the skies
    On flowery beds of ease,
While others fought to win the prize
    And sailed through bloody seas?

Are there no foes for me to face?
    Must I not stem the flood?
Is this vile world a friend to grace,
    To help me on to God!

Since I must fight if I would reign,
    Increase my courage, Lord!
I'll bear the toil, endure the pain,
    Supported by Thy word.

Isaac Watts

Benediction

*"For yours is the kingdom and the power
and the glory forever. Amen."*

For centuries, Christian congregations praying the Lord's Prayer have concluded with this benediction, and it is a fitting way to end such a wonderful prayer. Without it, our praying would begin with the Father and end with the devil. We would be moving from heaven to hell in a very short time, and that kind of liturgy is far from edifying. The benediction enables us to begin with the Lord, continue with the Lord, and end with the Lord.

However, scholars tell us that this benediction is not part of the original text and that it was probably added when churches began to pray the Lord's Prayer together in public worship. In the *Didache*, a second-century local church manual, it reads, "For thine is the power and the glory forever." Other manuscripts of Matthew's Gospel have different versions or no benediction at all.

Just because this benediction is not part of the original text doesn't mean that using it is a sin or that the benediction itself teaches heresy. It's generally agreed that the benediction is based on the words of David in 1 Chronicles 29 when he commissioned his son Solomon to build the temple.

Praise be to you, LORD, the God of our father Israel, from everlasting to everlasting. Yours, LORD, is the greatness and the power and the glory and the majesty and the splendor, for everything in heaven and earth is yours. Yours, LORD, is the kingdom; you are exalted as head over all. Wealth and honor come from you; you are the ruler of all things. In your hands are strength and power to exalt and to give strength to all. Now, our God, we give you thanks, and praise your glorious name.

1 Chronicles 29:10–13

The phrases "the kingdom" and "the power and the glory" are found here in David's magnificent expression of worship, as well as the phrase "from everlasting to everlasting." It's likely that the benediction in Matthew 6:13 was born out of this womb of inspired Scripture and therefore may be used by God's people today.

The statement "the kingdom and the power and the glory forever" is a poetical way of saying "your powerful glorious eternal kingdom," and it reminds us that our heavenly Father is wonderful beyond description. We can pray to him and praise him from grateful hearts, because prayer and praise go together. We open the Lord's Prayer with "Hallowed be your name," and we close it with "For yours is the kingdom and the power and the glory forever." True worship involves praise wrapped in prayer. That's the best way to keep our praying from being selfish.

The benediction begins with the word *for*, which suggests that it is an argument for this prayer and a defense of prayer itself. It says to us, "Prayer is reasonable." Why should we ask for these blessings? Because our God has willed to give them to those who ask and he is able to do what he wills. If he is King, he has power, and he reveals his glory to us by answering prayer. Satan wants to convince us that prayer is a waste of time, but the Word of God and our own Christian experience assure us that prayer is the key to God's treasury of grace.

The Lord's Prayer reveals to us what our God is like, and this should encourage us to pray. He is a Father who loves us and a King who reigns in heaven and works on earth. He provides our daily needs and forgives our sins. He guides us as we do his will and protects and delivers when the enemy attacks. Why should we worry or be afraid?

But the prayer not only reveals truth about God; it reveals truth about God's children. We are part of a glorious family ("*our* Father") that transcends time and space and one day will be gathered in heaven. Our sins are forgiven, and we have the blessed hope of sharing in Christ's promised kingdom. We depend on our Father to feed us and to lead us as we seek his will and obey it. Praying this prayer should remind us of our own needs (not our greeds!) and our Father's gracious provision. Above all else, it reminds us that all the glory belongs to the Lord, and that we should never ask the Father for anything that does not glorify him.

The phrase "yours is the kingdom" acknowledges that the Lord is in control and we must yield to his will. The command "Be still, and know that I am God" (Ps. 46:10) literally means, "Take your hands off. Relax!" We are too prone to tell the Father what to do and to start manipulating circumstances to suit ourselves, when we should submit to him because the kingdom is his. At times we walk by sight and wonder if God is at work at all, but this posture is both foolish and dangerous. Imagine how disturbed Mary and Martha were when Jesus delayed arriving at Bethany when their brother Lazarus was so sick. Our Lord waited so long that Lazarus died; but when Jesus raised him from the dead, it brought more glory to God than if he had simply healed him, and many people trusted Christ as a result.

When I was in confirmation class, I was taught that Jesus was a Prophet when he was on earth, he is a Priest now in heaven, and he will be King when he returns; but this is faulty theology. Today in heaven he is the King-Priest, a priest on a throne! Because he is a priest, he has sympathy for his people. And because he is a king, he has sovereignty to work on their behalf. For his people, his throne is a throne of grace, not a throne of judgment. "The LORD has established his throne in heaven, and his kingdom rules over all" (Ps. 103:19).

We must not minimize the phrase "and the power," for there are kings and queens who reign but cannot rule because they have no power or authority. They are primarily figure-heads, symbols of an ancient kingdom that help to "glue" things together. Our God is not like that. The angel Gabriel proclaimed to Mary, "For no word from God will ever fail" (Luke 1:37). And Jesus himself told his disciples that "all things are possible with God" (Mark 10:27). He has power! We see evidence of it in the world around us as well as in the functioning of our own bodies. The Word records what God did through the lives of believing people—Hebrews 11 is a good example—and challenges us to trust him to do in and through us that which will glorify him. "Very truly I tell you," said Jesus, "all who have faith in me will do the works I have been doing, and they will do even greater things than these, because I am going to the Father. And I will do whatever you ask in my name, so that the Father may be glorified in the Son" (John 14:12–13). What an encouragement to people who pray!

Let's be careful not to limit the demonstration of God's power to physical healing or the provision of material needs, because we need his power for overcoming the enemy, building character, and using our gifts and abilities to accomplish his will on earth. Jesus told us that, no matter how hard we try, apart from him we can do nothing (John 15:5). From writing a letter to preaching a sermon to performing an appendectomy, believers need the power of God. Only through the power of God will our ministry bring glory to God. As Paul extols in Ephesians 3:20–21, "Now to him who is able to do immeasurably more than all we ask or imagine, according to his power that is at work within us, to him be glory in the church and in Christ Jesus throughout all generations, for ever and ever! Amen."

That brings us to the next part of our benediction.

"For yours is the kingdom and the power *and the glory* . . ."

The Scriptures emphasize the fact that humanity is sinful and fragile and has no lasting glory. "All people are like grass, and all human faithfulness is like the flowers of the field. The grass withers and the flowers fall, because the breath of the LORD blows on them. Surely the people are grass. The grass withers and the flowers fall, but the word of our God endures forever" (Isa. 40:6–8).

I have four thick books in my library titled *Who Was Who*, published years ago by the same people who publish the well-known Who's Who series. The first volume begins with 1607 and the last one goes up to 1960. Occasionally I leaf through one of these volumes and look at the biographies of famous people, very few of whom I recognize. In their day, these people blossomed and attracted attention, but then their blossoms fell and their lives withered. Now they are remembered by only a few historians and other antiquarian specialists. Each time I walk into my library I see those four books and am reminded that my life is fragile and transient; only the Lord can make anything lasting out of it. "The world and its desires pass away, but whoever does the will of God lives forever" (1 John 2:17).

The kingdom belongs to God, the power belongs to God, and all the glory belongs to God. *But everyone who has trusted Jesus Christ also belongs to God!* Our Father wants to use our witness to bring others into the kingdom, to introduce them to the power of God that can change lives. Ephesians 3:20 points out that God's power works *in us*—ordinary people—and not just in the apostles. No doubt you have noticed that some television advertising includes a small line that reads, "This is a paid endorsement." Our witness for Christ is a "paid endorsement," because we have been "bought with a price," the blood of Jesus Christ. In fact, the price is a part of our witness!

God's power is available to us if we truly seek to do his will and glorify his name.

There is an awesomeness about the word *forever*—"the kingdom and the power and the glory forever." Even though we often pray about material and physical things that don't last forever, we are still dealing with the things of eternity that do last forever. Our prayers involve the will and the glory of our eternal God, and they are marked FOREVER. God is the eternal King, and his kingdom is "an everlasting kingdom" (Ps. 145:13). Prayer is not a waste of time; it is the best way to gain victory over time and invest in eternity. God has "set eternity in the human heart" (Eccles. 3:11), which helps to explain why unsaved people are dissatisfied with life. As they see family members and friends die, and as familiar landmarks crumble and organizations come and go, they crave permanence, but there is none. There can be no satisfaction or peace except in Jesus Christ, the eternal Son of God.

In Jesus we have eternal life, which is not simply "endless life," for lost souls in hell will exist endlessly. No, eternal life is the very life of God that is imparted to us when we trust Christ. While hell is an endless death, heaven is the experience of God's life forever. Possessing eternal life on earth now means living "days of heaven upon earth" (Deut. 11:21 KJV). Defining eternity is hard enough; comprehending it is even more difficult. "Time out of mind" says one dictionary, and another says "duration of time without beginning or ending." Because God is eternal, he had no beginning and will have no ending. "God dwells in eternity," wrote A. W. Tozer, "but time dwells in him."[32] We are a part of eternity because we have received eternal life—God's life—through faith in Jesus Christ. Eternal life dwells in us, and the Holy Spirit gives us a foretaste of heaven as we yield to him.

The Christian life is built on the eternal. The eternal God is our refuge (Deut. 33:27), and we rest on his eternal Word (Ps. 119:89). We will share in eternal glory (1 Peter 5:10) that far outweighs the burdens we carry today (2 Cor. 4:17). Each child of God will have a glorious new body, "an eternal house in heaven" (2 Cor. 5:1). We have an eternal inheritance that can never fade away (Heb. 9:15). All these blessings and much more are ours because we possess eternal life in Jesus Christ.

Consider the word *forever*. We will enjoy God's house— heaven—*forever* (Ps. 23:6). God's love endures *forever* (Psalm 136). He is faithful *forever* (Ps. 146:6). If we have been faithful, we will receive a crown that will last *forever* (1 Cor. 9:25). Through Jesus Christ, we have been "made perfect *forever*" (Heb. 10:14). God's Word stands *forever* (1 Peter 1:25).

Interestingly, in the New Testament epistles the word *amen* is linked with the words *glory* and *forever* a number of times (Rom. 11:36; Gal. 1:5; Eph. 3:21; Phil. 4:20; 1 Tim. 1:17; 2 Tim. 4:18; Heb. 13:21; 1 Peter 4:11 and 5:11; 2 Peter 3:18; Jude 25). Read these verses and meditate on them. As you do, rejoice in the fact that God's people are a part of eternity and will enjoy it forever!

C. S. Lewis wrote in *The Four Loves*, "All that is not eternal is eternally out of date."[33] We Christians are often called "old-fashioned" or "not with it" or "outdated" by people who don't know Christ, when actually *it is our accusers who are out of date*! Because we share in God's eternal life, the passage of time takes nothing away from us that really is essential. "Therefore we do not lose heart. Though outwardly we are wasting away, yet inwardly we are being renewed day by day" (2 Cor. 4:16). "So we fix our eyes not on what is seen, but on what is unseen, since what is seen is temporary, but what is unseen is eternal" (2 Cor. 4:18). Like the patriarchs of old, we live above the perishable by focusing on the eternal (Heb. 11:16).

"Aim at heaven," wrote C. S. Lewis, "and you will get earth 'thrown in': aim at earth and you will get neither."[34]

There are three words that Christian people throughout this world understand and use: *Jesus* ("Savior"), *hallelujah* ("praise the Lord"), and *amen* ("may it be so" or "may it come true"). Since Old Testament days, God's people have used the word *amen* as a response of faith and confidence to prayers, sermons, testimonies, and even songs. At Mount Ebal, where Moses led the nation of Israel in accepting God's covenant, they responded by saying "Amen!" to each blessing or curse (see Deuteronomy 27). Paul used *amen* five times as he wrote his letter to the Romans (1:25; 9:5; 11:36; 15:33; 16:27), and the apostle John wrote *amen* eight times in the book of Revelation (1:6, 7; 3:14; 5:14; 7:12; 19:4; 22:20, 21). Those verses are worth studying. In the early church, it was expected that worshipers would be led by the Spirit to praise God and say "Amen!" as they understood the Word being shared (1 Cor. 14:13–17).

Saying "Amen" in a service can be overdone. A well-known Bible teacher, now in heaven, was teaching at a conference, and a man sitting in the balcony kept shouting "Amen!" in response to almost every sentence the speaker uttered. The preacher, wearied of these distractions and interruptions, looked up at the man and said, "My brother, the Holy Spirit is a dove, not a hoot owl." That solved the problem. However, our problem today is just the opposite. Too many worshipers remain silent when they ought to express their faith more enthusiastically (without becoming hoot owls).

Over the centuries, Christian congregations have prayed the Lord's Prayer together and ended with a united "Amen." The word itself comes from the Hebrew and means "to lean on something strong to steady yourself." The image is one of a pilgrim leaning on his staff, or a person being protected and held up by a friend. *Amen* is related to words like *believe, trust, faithful, certain, reliable.* When we say "Amen!" to a preacher's statement, we're saying "Let it be so!" We're committing ourselves to the truth we just heard, and we want others to join us in this commitment.

The first occurrence of *amen* in the Bible is in Genesis 15:6: "Abram believed the LORD, and he credited it to him as righteousness." Literally the verse says, "Abram said 'Amen' to the Lord." The "amen" was his faith response to the promises of God in verses 1–5 (see Rom. 4:3, Gal. 3:6, and James 2:23). Abram was saying to the Lord, "Let it be so! May it come true!" He was affirming his confidence that God's promises were right and dependable and he didn't have to worry.

A "first cousin" of the Hebrew word *amen* is *emet*, which means "truth." "He who is blessed in the earth will be blessed by the God of truth; and he who swears in the earth will swear by the God of truth" (Isa. 65:16 NASB). In this verse, the Lord could be called "the God of the amen." To emphasize a statement, Jesus sometimes prefaced it with "Verily, verily" or "Truly, truly" (e.g., John 1:51; 5:19, 24, 25; 6:26, 32, 47). His words could very well be translated "Amen, amen."

One of the names of Jesus is "the Amen" (Rev. 3:14). Paul's words in 2 Corinthians 1:20 help us understand and apply this name: "For no matter how many promises God has made, they are 'Yes' in Christ. And so through him the 'Amen' is spoken by us to the glory of God." The promises the Father has given to his people, he first gave to his Son, *and the Father will never violate those promises*! When by faith we say "Amen!" to a promise and claim it in the name of Jesus, that promise will be honored to the glory of God.

As we abide in Christ, the Spirit shows us the promises in the Word that we need. We claim these promises by faith when we say "Amen!" through Jesus Christ, because Jesus is the Father's "Amen" to every promise that we need. The deeper we go into the Scriptures, the better we get to know our Savior and the promises we have in him. Like Abraham, we must hear God's promise and say "Amen!" to it as we claim it for ourselves.

Jesus Christ is the Father's Amen *to* us and guarantees each promise. He is also the Amen *for* us as he intercedes for us before the throne. But even more, Jesus is God's Amen *in* us through the Holy Spirit, teaching us, assuring us, and enabling us to say "Amen" to our Lord's "Yes" in Christ (2 Cor. 1:20). We enjoy all these privileges as we pray and fellowship with God.

As unbelievable as it sounds, here on earth we are sharing in eternity! That's why the words *kingdom, power, glory, forever,* and *amen* are so important. They help us to take inventory so we can make sure we are "on praying ground."

Kingdom—Am I a faithful child and servant of the King?

Power—Am I depending on his power as I serve him?

Glory—Is my motive only to glorify Jesus Christ?

Forever—Do I live with eternity's values in view?

Amen—Am I walking by faith and saying "Amen!" to his promises?

If we can answer "yes" to the above questions, then we are privileged to share in eternity as we pray.

Prayer Is the Soul's Sincere Desire

Prayer is the soul's sincere desire,
Unuttered or expressed,
The motion of a hidden fire
That trembles in the breast.

Prayer is the burden of a sigh,
The falling of a tear,
The upward glancing of an eye
When none but God is near.

Prayer is the simplest form of speech
That infant lips can try;
Prayer, the sublimest strains that reach
The Majesty on high.

Prayer is the Christian's vital breath,
The Christian's native air,
His watchword at the gates of death;
He enters heaven with prayer.

O Thou, by whom we come to God,
The Life, the Truth, the Way,
The path of prayer Thyself hast trod;
Lord, teach us how to pray.

James Montgomery

Notes

1. *The Table Talk of Martin Luther*, ed. Thomas S. Kepler (Grand Rapids: Baker, 1979), 202.

2. P. T. Forsyth, *The Soul of Prayer* (London: Charles H. Kelly, 1916), 10.

3. Alexander Whyte, *Teach Us To Pray* (London: Hodder & Stoughton, 1922), 15. Whyte uses the word *men* generically to include all believers, both men and women.

4. Ibid., 51.

5. C. H. Spurgeon, *Autobiography: The Early Years* (London: Banner of Truth Trust, n.d.), 390. The reference is to Rev. 1:13–16.

6. The Lord's Prayer is also called the Disciples' Prayer and the Our Father (*Pater Noster* in Latin). The benediction ("For yours is the kingdom") is not found in leading ancient manuscripts.

7. Some students see seven requests. However, the conjunction *but* in v. 13 probably indicates that "lead us not" and "deliver us" are part of the same request, to overcome the enemy, Satan.

8. John W. Doberstein, ed., *Minister's Prayer Book* (Philadelphia: Fortress, 1959), 445–46.

9. Millard J. Erickson, *Christian Theology*, one volume edition (Grand Rapids: Baker, 1987), 313–14.

10. Our Lord's promise in Luke 11:9–10 covers God's wealth ("ask"), God's will ("seek"), and God's work ("knock"). In Scripture, an open door is a metaphor for an opportunity to serve God (1 Cor. 16:8–9).

11. Thomas Merton, *New Seeds of Contemplation* (New York: New Direction Books, 1961), 53.

12. See Carl B. Hoch Jr., *All Things New* (Grand Rapids: Baker, 1995), 248–50; and the trilogy by Gene Getz, *Building Up One Another*, *Loving One Another*, and *Encouraging One Another* (Colorado Springs: Victor, 2002).

13. Forsyth, *The Soul of Prayer*, 114.

14. G. Campbell Morgan, *The Teaching of Christ* (Old Tappan, NJ: Revell, 1913), 204.

15. Ibid., 219.

16. Robert Law, *The Tests of Life* (Edinburgh: T & T Clark, 1909), 304.

17. Note the requests in these references: Rom. 15:30–33; 2 Cor. 1:8–11; Eph. 6:18–19; Phil. 1:19; Col. 4:3; 1 Thess. 5:25; 2 Thess. 3:1; Philem. 22.

18. Law, *The Tests of Life*, 304.

19. Forsyth, *The Soul of Prayer*, 48–49.

20. Ibid., 51.

21. Tony Castle, ed., *The New Book of Christian Quotations* (New York: Crossroads, 1984), 191.

22. Forsyth, *The Soul of Prayer*, 56.

23. It's not likely that Jesus was speaking in John 6 about the Lord's Supper or Eucharist. He hadn't even discussed that subject with his own disciples, so why would he speak of it to a crowd of unbelieving Jews? John 6:63 makes it clear that it is the Spirit who gives life, not material bread.

24. "Day by Day and with Each Passing Moment" by Carolina Sandell Berg, translated by Andrew L. Skoog.

25. Charles Haddon Spurgeon, *The Metropolitan Tabernacle Pulpit* (Pasadena, TX: Pilgrim Publications, 1988), vol. 35, 217.

26. P. T. Forsyth, *Positive Preaching and the Modern Mind* (London: Independent Press, 1953), 28.

27. Forsyth, *The Soul of Prayer*, 58.

28. See my book *50 People Every Christian Should Know* (Grand Rapids: Baker, 2008). This is a new and expanded edition of my previous book *Living with the Giants*.

29. Charles H. Spurgeon, *Commenting and Commentaries* (London: Banner of Truth Trust, 1969), 1.

30. For a detailed exposition of the four appearances of the devil in the Old Testament, see my book *The Strategy of Satan* (Carol Stream, IL: Tyndale, 1979).

31. Charles Haddon Spurgeon, *The Metropolitan Tabernacle Pulpit* (Pasadena, TX: Pilgrim Publications, 1980), vol. 26, 224.

32. A. W. Tozer, *The Knowledge of the Holy* (New York: Harper, 1961), 45.

33. C. S. Lewis, *The Four Loves* (New York: Harcourt, 1960), 137.

34. C. S. Lewis, *Mere Christianity* (New York: Macmillan, 1960), 104.

Warren W. Wiersbe is a former pastor of the Moody Church and author or editor of more than 150 books, including *On Being a Servant of God* and *The Bumps Are What You Climb On*. He lives with his wife, Betty, in Lincoln, Nebraska, where he continues to write and to mentor younger pastors.

Also by

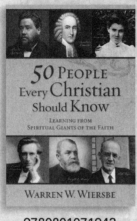

9780801071942

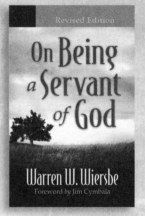

9780801068195

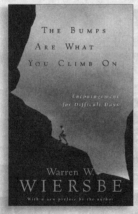

9780801064425

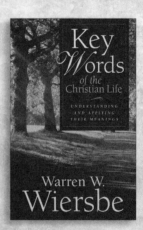

9780801064319

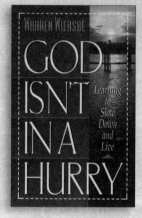
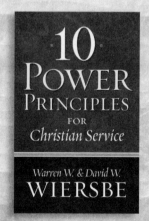